# Better Than OK

# Better Than OK

## Finding Joy as a Special-Needs Parent

## KELLY MANTOAN

Our Sunday Visitor
Huntington, Indiana

Our Sunday Visitor Publishing Division
Our Sunday Visitor, Inc.
200 Noll Plaza
Huntington, IN 46750
1-800-348-2440

ISBN: 978-1-68192-416-8 (Inventory No. T2310)
eISBN: 978-1-68192-417-5
LCCN: 2021938261

Cover design: Chelsea Alt
Cover art: Adobe Stock
Interior design: Amanda Falk

PRINTED IN THE UNITED STATES OF AMERICA

*For my husband, Tony, with love.*

# Contents

# Contents

# Introduction

While on our way home from vacation in the summer of 2016, my husband, Tony, and I found ourselves weaving through a strange neighborhood to find a church for Sunday Mass. The houses around us became more and more derelict, but Google Maps directed us onward.

"Is this neighborhood safe?"

"Where exactly are you taking us for Mass?"

"Will we make it before the Gospel reading?"

The litany of questions from the back seat was increasing in volume and length by the minute. I stared at the map on my phone and tried to navigate my husband through these last few turns without either of us losing our temper. Before long, the church stood in front of us, a traditional stone edifice amid a sea of crumbling homes and litter.

The neighborhood was quiet, with little traffic, so we parked our handicap van and trailer on the wrong side of the street and

Tony unloaded our sons' wheelchairs into the road. I scouted ahead for the handicap entrance, wondering if one even existed. Finally, I spotted it tucked around the side. We found a door that led to a small foyer with an old elevator. Our family of seven had to split into two trips to get to the chapel. I prayed we wouldn't make too much of a scene with our late arrival.

The door slid open and deposited us at the back of the nave where mothers chased toddlers, and ushers turned and smiled. We hadn't missed the Gospel, but there was nowhere to sit. So we stood in the back, my youngest sons parked in their wheelchairs, as out of the way as possible. We all quickly became uncomfortably aware of the fact that the air conditioning was not working.

I said a silent prayer thanking the Lord for getting us all to Mass in a mostly timely manner. I soon noticed a child lying on the rug near my feet, sucking on a pacifier, and I immediately recognized a long G-tube extension protruding from the leg hole of his onesie — which meant that he received at least some of his food through a special port in his stomach, just like my son Fulton. The boy's mother stood nearby and I smiled. We had something in common. My knee-jerk reaction as a mom to two children with a rare neuromuscular disorder, known as spinal muscular atrophy, meant that I couldn't help but consider a possible diagnosis: At the very least, his size and lack of crawling and walking probably indicated a gross motor delay.

I approached the mother at the end of Mass as she cradled him against her chest. "He's a cutie! How old is he?"

"This is Tim, and he's 18 months." She hesitated briefly before adding, "I'm Cindy. I read your blog. I don't know if you remember, but I emailed you recently about Tim once we realized he had the same diagnosis as my other son, Michael, who's sitting over there with his father."

Recognition dawned on me. I remembered her email. "Oh yes! I remember! How are your sons doing? How are *you* doing?"

Her answers were cut short by the people trying to file out of church and the pleas of Fulton and Teddy for permission to speed around the sanctuary, until she mentioned free doughnuts and coffee in the basement — just the incentive my family needed to stick around.

Having descended to the basement, my husband avoided making small talk by busying himself with the kids, who were trying to pilfer as many free doughnuts as possible. I quickly returned to my conversation with the young mother. Ever the extrovert, fueled on by a hot cup of coffee, I asked about the parish and the town. I talked about the family trip that had brought us to this part of the Midwest, and the grueling drive that still lay ahead. I tried to throw in some supportive words and advice, but I found it difficult to weave them into casual conversation. I don't recall saying anything particularly earth-shattering, though I understood and sympathized with the struggle this young woman and her family were facing.

When I noticed the big kids were looking for thirds, and Fulton and Teddy were starting to race faster and faster through the small, crowded church hall, Tony and I shared a glance and I knew it was time to go.

Once we arrived at home, and I got a good night's sleep under my belt, I jumped online and discovered a new email from Cindy nestled under our previous email exchange, which I'd saved to a special folder reserved for messages from blog readers, many of whom are struggling with a child's severe medical diagnosis. Cindy wrote, "My husband was so thankful to see your boys at Mass. Our four-year-old hasn't been doing very well and my husband has been having a hard time watching him decline. He commented that after seeing your boys in their chairs he feels more at peace and confident that Michael would be just fine in a wheelchair. Thank you for that!"

Her email gave me peace of mind because I had been worried about saying just the right thing. Although I try to be the model mom of kids with special needs and be on *my* best Mass behavior, no matter how loud or rowdy the boys may be in their chairs, that wasn't what this woman, or her husband, needed that day. They needed to see that the worst fears we have for our children aren't always as bad as we imagine them to be. Two happy boys in wheelchairs gave them just a bit more hope than they had before.

You just never know how God will use your words, your actions, your example, or just your family's presence to change or comfort hearts and minds.

When I first started sharing my struggles and joys online, I didn't know God was going to do anything with my blog. I thought I was documenting my growing family's days before they slipped by and I'd forgotten all the stories and laughter. I didn't know I was growing in grace and gaining experience that would change my heart and prepare me to help others.

In both instances, God had a plan far beyond mine. He used my words, even the misspelled ones stuck together with poor grammar, to reach people around the world. When the emails started arriving in my inbox, I thought the first couple were a fluke. Surely these people had more reliable sources for information and support than me! I'm just a mommy blogger with a disastrous kitchen and piles of laundry, who still couldn't reliably order medical supplies on schedule. Nevertheless, emails kept coming, and I realized that many times I was the only sliver of hope these people could find in the darkness of their child's diagnosis.

The realization of how God was using my blog was both humbling and scary. Every time I started typing out a reply, I said a prayer to the Holy Spirit to help me to respond with just the right words.

Most of my exchanges with parents only extend to a few

brief emails before I file the conversation in my email folder. I rarely meet them or learn whether or not the struggle has lessened, whether something I wrote helped them or offended them.

I can only speak to my experiences and how being a mom to children with special needs has changed me in ways I never anticipated. I thought I would be unhappy, tired, and filled with worry forever. I thought my sons would also be sad and focused on all the things they couldn't do. I expected my older children to be upset that their younger brothers were disabled, and jealous of all the time I spent with them.

But I was wrong. And I want all the parents who reach out to me, and those who pick up this book, to know that your future, and your child's, is only a dark and scary place if you let it become one. You can move past the initial stages of grief that are common after a special-needs diagnosis and arrive at acceptance and renewed faith. I've come to see there's no such thing as a perfect child, except in that every child is perfect just as they've been created. I learned my love is not limited by a diagnosis, and neither is my sons'.

As you read my story, you'll probably see great similarities to your own, regardless of your child's diagnosis. And hopefully you'll see that, just as I came through the dark valley after my sons' diagnoses, you can too. I'm not special or a saint. Accepting your child's diagnosis and finding renewed hope, gratitude, fortitude, perseverance, humility, charity, understanding, and prudence — and, ultimately, joy — amid all the challenges is possible for anyone. My story is unique, but my outcome is not. I am a stronger, more humble, sacrificial, and faith-filled person than I was before I started this journey. These have not always been easy lessons to learn, and many remain works in progress, but I hope that by sharing them, those of you feeling overwhelmed in similar situations may find guidance and encouragement. Overcoming grief and growing in these graces does not happen overnight. But give God space to work in your heart, and in time you will see how he has helped you arrive at a better, more joyful place than you are now.

# 1
# Learning from Our Children's Example

## *The Grace of Acceptance*

When our fourth child was diagnosed with a rare neuro-muscular disorder, my husband and I grieved the loss of the perfect life we'd envisioned for our family, and more specifically for our son. We had to learn to see our son as God saw him, and ultimately how our three other children viewed him as well.

That learning curve was not easy, but it was predictable. Most parents of children with special needs will likely go through identifiable stages following a special-needs diagnosis. My aim is to help you work through those stages, to overcome them through acceptance and childlike faith.

A special-needs diagnosis is not a literal death, but in hindsight I can see how I worked through, in true textbook fashion, all the stages of grief: shock, denial, anger, bargaining, and depression, with acceptance coming along at the end, when I was finally ready for it.

Years passed before I reached a place in my thoughts and in my heart where I could rejoice in my family and blog about the joys of family life, let alone extend those thoughts to give hope and encouragement to other parents in my position. The bottom line is that bad things happen to our children, but we don't need to stay trapped in sadness, anger, and despair. God wants more for us and for our children.

The Bible tells us that God doesn't call the qualified; he qualifies the called (see 1 Cor 1:27–29). Those of us called to parent special children with unique gifts and challenges can rise to meet these challenges in several ways, but I've found that by opening myself to God's grace, I've become the parent my boys needed much faster than through my earlier, unsuccessful efforts — which consisted primarily of complaining to God. I initially refused to accept the possibility that this life, as hard as it could be, might actually be wonderful. Rather than feeling that God's will had been forced upon my child and our family, I can now see how life's circumstances have strengthened me to be the woman God needs me to be to do his work.

We can do hard things. We can plod through them joylessly, or we can embrace whatever life has in store for us and allow it to grow our hearts and minds, and our relationship with God and those in our family and community. Being physically fit and healthy requires constant hard work. Being well-educated, or moving up the corporate ladder, requires hard work. Maintaining a clean home with happy kids requires hard work. Special-needs parenting is *hard*. Being an advocate, caregiver, and medical expert on top of everything else you do is extremely hard. But you can do it. And you don't need to do it alone. You can move past grief in all its forms and open yourself up to God's grace and all the ways he will help you carry his yoke.

What follows is the longest chapter in the book because it covers all the stages you are likely to experience, or are going through right now. Some will last longer than others, and some will overlap. It's not uncommon to think you've moved past a stage only to find yourself feeling a certain way again. I have broken up the chapter by providing tips at the end of each section that will help you navigate through each stage. Your goal should not be to skip any of these stages or avoid the grieving process altogether, but to recognize each one, admit your feelings, allow yourself to feel that way, understand why your child's diagnosis has triggered this feeling, and move forward in the healing and acceptance process, rather than allowing yourself to sit and wallow in any one stage. Learning about grief, and all its manifestations, is an important first step in moving forward with joy.

## Stage One: Shock

For months we had convinced ourselves that Fulton's gross motor delays were nothing to worry about — nothing a little more tummy time and less spoiling by his adoring family couldn't fix. It wasn't until an informal evaluation by a friendly neighbor that we realized more was going on.

I sat laughing, wine glass in hand, trying to enjoy another laid-back homeschool moms social hosted by my good friend Julie. Fulton, my seven-month-old son, lay on the floor smiling, playing with the toys in his hands and enjoying his role as the center of attention. A new mom showed up late and introduced herself to me. I motioned to my son on the floor and she inquired about his age.

"He's seven months."

"Wow, he's really happy just laying around for a seven-month-old!"

I forced a smile. "Yes, he's showing some motor delays. That's why I brought him. Julie's neighbor is a physical therapist, and he agreed to meet with me tonight and give him a quick look over."

I convinced myself it was nothing. Perhaps he just needed some physical therapy. I had three healthy children. There were no diseases on any branch of the family tree. Meeting with Julie's friend was just to reassure Tony and me that it was no big deal. When Dan arrived, I carried Fulton into the living room where Dan looked him over seriously. I kept waiting for the reassuring words.

"He has a lot of head lag. See how floppy his head is? And if I lower him to the floor like this, you'll notice he has no protective reflexes."

"What does that mean?"

"He should try to put his arms up to protect his face, but he doesn't." I watched as he quickly lowered Fulton to the floor face down and Fulton looked distressed, but didn't move his arms, or even lift his head away.

"We did notice his legs seem weak; he doesn't crawl or try to stand."

"He has muscle weakness all over, not just in his legs." He showed me where Fulton displayed stiffness and limited range of motion in his shoulders from lack of use. Finally, Dan looked up from my son and met my gaze. "You need to take him to a neurologist immediately."

I hesitated because I knew that would require a visit to the pediatrician for a referral. At Fulton's six-month well visit, the nurse practitioner who examined him noted his delays, but blamed me for not interacting with him enough. I tried to juggle my three older children, ages five, four, and two, in the exam room with exaggerated patience as she chastised me for ignoring my baby. Clearly I was in over my head with my large brood and could not provide enough of the tummy time, stimulation, and one-on-one interaction my baby needed. At the time, I simply brushed her off and made a mental note to never schedule an appointment with her again. Now I wondered if I would be able to convince a different doctor in the practice that Fulton really did need to see a specialist, based on this informal physical therapy evaluation.

I called to make a new appointment and told the scheduler our concerns. Within a few days, Fulton and I went by ourselves and saw a different doctor in the practice. Not only was this doctor alarmed at the delays, he immediately knew it wasn't a parenting issue. He pointed out in greater detail what he was concerned about, including the fact that Fulton had no reflexes. Repeated hammer hits to his knee were met with grumpy stares by my baby. I was stunned. How did no one pick up on this before? How could I have been so blind as to how far behind my son was in his physical development? I got my specialist appointment at the Children's Hospital of Philadelphia in no time. I tried to ignore the fact that everyone seemed so concerned and these appointments kept immediately opening up. Dr. Google was not helping either. Searches turned up scary things I'd heard of like muscular dystrophy and spina bifida, and scary things I'd never heard of and could hardly pronounce, like spinal muscular atrophy and mitochondrial diseases. I found myself hoping for spina bifida. It seemed the least threatening of the bunch. But I also held on to the belief that it would ultimately be nothing, or something that, with a little work, Fulton would outgrow.

Finally, my father-in-law drove Fulton and me downtown to the Children's Hospital of Philadelphia for our neuromuscular appointment. I tried to avoid looking at the other waiting patients, some with a physical disability. I worked to convince myself that we'd never need to return here like these families. Fulton and I were whisked back promptly to our appointment and I described the symptoms to the intake nurse, then doctor. After only a quick examination, and much to my surprise, they wanted to admit him to the hospital for testing. At every turn, we kept waiting for the news that it wasn't a big deal, yet we kept moving in the opposite direction.

As I retold all the details of the first year of his life over and over during that first overnight stay, I wondered if I'd been overlooking too much. I started to question my ability as a mother. Shouldn't I have known sooner to bring him to a specialist? As each new medical professional entered the room, none would reassure me that it was nothing. All I wanted was for one doctor to tell me not to worry, or smile and say everything would turn out fine, but those words never came. Fulton's symptoms were confusing and tough to pin on one specific condition. Once they determined he wasn't in immediate danger, he was discharged with testing to continue on an outpatient basis. When the muscle ultrasound seemed to rule out muscular dystrophy, they told me they would test him for spinal muscular atrophy (SMA), just to rule it out, and call me with results in a week. The neuromuscular resident smiled and added that the doctor who specialized in SMA didn't think it was SMA because Fulton didn't exhibit certain symptoms. I was relieved we could check that off the list.

But a week later, when the results came in, we were given the shock of our lives when a medical fellow told me over the phone that the genetic test done to rule out SMA actually confirmed my son's diagnosis.

Two days later, my husband and I were back at the hospital with the doctor who originally didn't think our son presented the symptoms of SMA, now telling us Fulton had a disease that was like "Lou Gehrig's disease for children." I could barely follow the doctor's endless stream of medical jargon about genetics and proteins before he suggested joining a drug trial at Johns Hopkins Hospital in Baltimore, Maryland. My head was spinning. Fulton laid on the table and happily allowed himself to be prodded for the millionth time since we had started trying to get answers four months prior. We were only a couple of weeks away from his first birthday, and instead of preparing for a big party, my husband and I prepared to accept a diagnosis that killed 60 percent of children diagnosed before their third birthday.

We finally had answers, but they were much worse than anything we could have imagined. Children with SMA fall into four types — with type 1 the most common and most severe, usually diagnosed shortly after birth, up to type 4, which is rare and appears in adulthood. Fulton was considered a strong type 1 or weak type 2. He didn't require any respiratory support and could eat all his food orally. Although he couldn't move like a typical eleven-month-old, he could sit with assistance, roll from side to side, and thankfully SMA couldn't and wouldn't steal his joyful, carefree attitude. But children with SMA become weaker over time, gradually losing all voluntary muscle movement until they require complete support to breathe, communicate, move, and eat. Respiratory infections are dangerous for kids with SMA because all-over muscle weakness makes it difficult to clear their lungs and airways, making pneumonia a constant threat during the winter. A weak swallow can also lead to the accidental aspiration of fluid or food into the lungs and pneumonia. Scoliosis, or curvature of the spine, is common, and often treated with surgery. There is no way to predict how fast the disease will rob a child of his physical abilities.

Fulton would be completely dependent on other people to care for him his entire life. There were no cures, and only a few treatment options that showed inconsistent results. He would need continual physical and occupational therapy to keep what abilities he did have, and to prevent stiffness. Fulton would require a power wheelchair, and a van and home to accommodate it. His second-floor bedroom, in the home we'd purchased less than a year prior, wouldn't do.

Overnight, our lives changed. It was as if we'd won the absolute worst lottery ever. We couldn't believe our son was the one in six thousand children diagnosed with SMA. The vastness of this prize was so large and overwhelming we couldn't comprehend all the ways in which it would change our lives. Neither of us knew anyone who was physically disabled, save for some distant or elderly relatives. We weren't close with anyone who was parenting a child with a major medical condition. My experience with special-needs children was limited to babysitting a child with Down syndrome when I was twelve.

I cried in those first few days after the diagnosis, even though I struggled to wrap my head around what we were facing. The diagnosis so completely surprised us and came out of left field that we were dazed and confused. If I happened to take my mind off the diagnosis for a while, when it entered my mind again, it was almost like a fresh slap to the face.

As I relayed the message to friends and family, I became familiar with the look of horror and pain that would quickly spread across their faces. Since we started trying to get to the bottom of Fulton's motor delays, I'd updated people through social media, and each time people responded with prayers and encouraging words. So when I had to share the worst possible news, everyone was shocked. My father was even outraged, suspecting that the hospital had messed up the genetic test and wondering out loud if we should get it retaken. Everyone, Tony and myself included, had worked hard to convince themselves that everything would be fine, so hard that, faced with the opposite, they were left speechless. Some, like my father, even still tried to convince me that it was a mistake, that doctors didn't know everything, and that Fulton might be just fine. It was hard to insist that he wouldn't be fine and the test was correct; Fulton had a devastating medical condition with no cure. I struggled to get the words out of my mouth. I needed people to believe what I was saying and console me because I was still in shock and struggling to believe the words myself.

If your child's diagnosis blindsided you, know that a special-needs diagnosis is not on the radar for anyone. Whether it's diagnosed in utero or after birth, there is no anticipating its arrival. Three typical children did not protect me from becoming a special-needs parent. And even when I meditated on parenting and envisioned what I could handle, the most I could imagine was a child with a learning disability or maybe Down syndrome. Thinking about those first few days post-diagnosis will always stir up emotions, and the anniversary of that phone call is etched in my mind. I will never forget that difficult time and those first feelings of disbelief, no matter how many years pass.

## What You Can Do: Handling the Shock

Understand that this stage will move quickly, and overlap with the next stages. Don't bottle up any emotions that may rise to the surface as you grapple with the news. You may feel numb for a while, travel through the days in a haze, and not remember one hour from the next. Whatever emotions do rise to the surface in the early days, consider writing them down in a private journal, finding a close friend or mental health counselor you can speak to who knows to simply listen, or find a safe place to release your tears, screams, or any physical manifestations (I used to punch my bed, or ugly cry into my pillow).

Your shock is unique, but the news of your child's diagnosis will resonate much farther than just your immediate family. If you are still in shock, you do not need to break the news personally to every single person, and you can request privacy as you deal with the information. It is not your responsibility to help everyone else process their own shock. When someone suddenly dies, it's customary for an employer to give an employee several days off; you, as a parent, are entitled to take time off too. Do not feel bad stepping aside from work or outside commitments for the first few days post-diagnosis. Designate a trusted friend or family member to let people know about your child's diagnosis, or post on social media for you. Limit your intake of information; gather what resources are given to you by doctors, specialists, case managers, etc., but you don't need to read and understand it all at this point. Set all that aside for later.

Imagine the shock felt by Mary as she met her son on the way to Calvary. Here was her only son, almost unrecognizable from the treatment he endured at the hands of his captors. And imagine the shock felt by the women who went to visit Jesus in the tomb, only to find the stone rolled away and the tomb empty. Those closest to Christ have suffered some of the greatest losses. We can turn to the first followers of Our Lord and ask for their prayers as we deal with this unbelievable diagnosis just given to our child. After the shock of the crucifixion and the empty tomb, the apostles enjoyed the Lord's resurrection and ascension, but this did not mean they were spared suffering. They went forth and did the work laid before them with all the graces we'll cover in this book.

Know that the shock you feel now will pass, and while it may seem hard to believe, you can be strengthened by God's grace for the path ahead. This is the beginning, and it is in many ways the hardest part, but it is a temporary season. Know that while things may get harder before they get better, the big picture is much brighter than what you can imagine right now.

---

## KEY TAKEAWAYS

- The stage of shock will pass quickly.
- Designate a friend or family member to share the diagnosis with others, if telling people yourself is

too difficult.

- Take time off work, or step away from outside responsibilities, for at least a few days post-diagnosis.
- Save all the information given to you by doctors and specialists, but save it to read at a future time when you can give it the attention it deserves.

## Prayer to Our Lady of Sorrows

Our Mother of Sorrows, with strength from above you stood by the cross, sharing in the sufferings of Jesus, and with tender care you bore him in your arms, mourning and weeping.

We praise you for your faith, which accepted the life God planned for you. We praise you for your hope, which trusted that God would do great things in you. We praise you for your love in bearing with Jesus the sorrows of his passion.

Holy Mary, may we follow your example, and stand by all your children who need comfort and love.

Mother of God, stand by us in our trials and care for us in our many needs. Pray for us now and at the hour of our death. Amen.*

## Stage Two: Denial

Once we had the diagnosis, I went back to the pediatrician for Fulton's one-year-old well visit. I scheduled the appointment with the same doctor who had sent us to the specialist. He had been sent the copy of the genetic test, and so in examining Fulton we both knew why he wasn't able to do what most one-year-olds could do. I filled him in on all the appointments in the works, and toward the end of the appointment he handed me a slip of paper.

---

*https://www.catholic.org/prayers/prayer.php?p=2456.

"This is a mom I know with a child who had SMA. He's passed away, but she might still be a resource for you."

Soon after at church, a friend approached me and said she knew someone whose daughter had SMA, but she hesitated to give me the name since this mother had left the Faith and she and her husband had divorced due to her daughter's health and related caregiving. The daughter required a feeding tube, a ventilator, and couldn't do anything independently. My friend wasn't sure if I'd want to talk to this mom, but she could get me her info if I was interested.

When our parish priest talked to us, he expressed his sorrow and said he didn't realize SMA was even a possibility for Fulton. The only time he'd heard of SMA was when another parishioner's grandson died within a few months of his birth from the disease.

And so it continued for the first few months after Fulton's diagnosis. Most people had never heard of SMA, but those who did often only knew of a child who had died, or was much more severely affected. I started to dread telling acquaintances because no one seemed to offer anything but sad stories.

In a couple of weeks, when we started receiving a magazine from a large SMA charity, I quickly threw it away to avoid looking at the large memorial section that documented dozens of kids each month who had died from the disease. Talking to other SMA families terrified me because I would be forced to confront all the worst parts of the disease. I felt like I already knew too much and couldn't handle any more bad news they might have to share.

The same SMA charity held a conference every year, and newly diagnosed families could attend for free. As I looked at the upcoming announcements and photos on the magazine cover, I balked. How could I explain to Fulton's siblings that the children pictured within — on ventilators and pushed in strollers laden with medical tubing and supplies — could someday be their brother? How could I bear to look at pictures of children, teenagers, and adults whose bodies were curved from scoliosis and dependent on machinery to move, breathe, and eat, and know that was the future in store for my child? I couldn't. I couldn't deny that something was wrong with my son, but I could deny that it would change our family now, or down the road. Those children were not my son, even though the genetic results said otherwise. He would never look like that, and I would never be one of those parents pictured with a smile on their face, at a conference full of other parents, happy to spread awareness and talk SMA nonstop.

When Fulton was accepted into a drug trial at Johns Hopkins in Baltimore, I met my first representative from the Muscular Dystrophy Association. Since SMA is a neuromuscular disease, the MDA provides services to SMA families. Despite the rep's friendly smile and persistence, I refused any assistance with meeting other SMA or MDA families.

But other doctors, nurses, therapists, and social workers couldn't let it go. At every appointment at Johns Hopkins or Children's Hospital I was asked if I'd connected with other special-needs or SMA parents. Did I want to be introduced to someone whose child, usually, had died of SMA? NO, THANK YOU.

I took the scraps of paper with phone numbers and names, all so carefully written down, and shoved them in a bin of papers and ignored them. I didn't call any of the contacts people gave me. I didn't read any of the literature sent to me by SMA organizations or handed to me by doctors. I refused to call myself an SMA mom or mother of a child with special needs. I didn't know what the future held, so I avoided thinking about it at all costs. Instead, I tried to maintain the same rhythm and routine we'd always had in our home, even as Fulton required more care, more equipment, and more appointments. We had created a wonder-

ful family, and I hoped that by closing my eyes and ignoring other SMA families I could pretend that nothing out of the ordinary
lay down the road.

I was quite sure I didn't need a special group of people to
talk to. Those people would certainly force me to face how awful
this disease was and then require me to discuss it in detail. I preferred to remain in my bubble, viewing SMA only through the
lens of my family, and special-needs parenting as only one tiny
sliver of all the other parenting I was already doing.

As long as I avoided talking to other parents, I didn't need
to face the reality of SMA. I could believe that everything would
remain the same in our family and that nothing would arise that
I couldn't handle. As if my six years of parenting had prepared
me for whatever medical calamity Fulton would present. I could
believe I would be strong enough, my marriage would be strong
enough, and everything would be fine. We would handle SMA the
Mantoan way, which we would just make up as we went along.

As a type A person, a planner, and a list writer, I wanted
complete control over my life. When problems arose I wanted
to quickly figure out a solution, make a plan, and move forward.
Facing spinal muscular atrophy destroyed my sense of control;
the disease meandered and created damage at its own unpredict-
able pace. With no cure and no reliable treatments at the time,
the progression of the disease was completely out of my hands.
I had no way to know what the future would look like for Fulton. This wild, uncontrollable uncertainty reminded me that I
was not in control, God was; but that didn't mean I would get
custom-engraved stone tablets telling me what to expect or how
to prepare. I quickly went into denial to try to forget how little
control I had over the situation.

But of course, SMA was here to stay whether I wanted to
look it in the face or not. By denying the severity of SMA, I
thought I was in control of the situation, but I wasn't, because I

was still faced with a disabled child whose needs were unlike my other children's in significant ways.

## What You Can Do: Taming Denial

Even when presented with a clear-cut test result with 99.99 percent accuracy, we can turn a blind eye to the symptoms and struggles our child is facing, or will face in the near future. Repeating the refrain, "Not our child, not our family," over and over in our head distances us from the truth in front of our faces.

Our Lord appeared in the Upper Room with his apostles, but Thomas wasn't there, so he didn't believe his friends. Thomas denied the Resurrection and claimed he could not believe until he put his hand in Jesus' side and his fingers in the nail holes. What reason had he to doubt? Didn't he trust the other apostles? Didn't he believe Jesus would do as he had promised?

What reason have you to deny your child's diagnosis, besides your desire to preserve your life as it is and maintain a predictable future path for your family? Christ's resurrection upended Thomas's life and the whole world. As much as Thomas wanted to preserve his life as he knew it, Jesus' invitation to put his hand in the Lord's side forced Thomas to admit that things could not be as they were before. As painful as loss of control and uncertainty is, denial only prolongs a false sense of control and temporarily disguises our fear.

Avoiding doctors, appointments, and other parents whose children have the same condition doesn't mean your child is no longer disabled. It simply means you are in denial. Refusing a "label" or making excuses for your child's behavior or lack of abilities is not protecting them. It's holding them back from the help they need, and it's holding you back from acceptance. Connecting with people and becoming educated is not throwing your hands up in defeat and resigning yourself to worst-case scenarios. It is being led down the path to wisdom. Denial seeks to remain ignorant, and in the process cuts itself off from hope, because it can't imagine joy outside a preconceived narrative of what family life should look like.

Saint Peter denied Our Lord three times, just as Jesus predicted, because he was afraid of what would happen if he admitted to being a follower of Christ. Once the cock crowed, he immediately regretted his behavior, recognized that his actions were motivated by fear, and knew he had acted contrary to his love of Our Lord.

Fear also sits at the root of your denial — fear of the unknown and a fear of being out of control of a situation. Recognize that by allowing yourself to be motivated by fear, you too may actually be withholding the love and care your child needs. It's OK to admit you're scared. It's OK to say you don't know what to do next. It's OK to view an uncertain future with hesitancy. These are all normal feelings, but like Thomas and Peter, we must recognize our fear and seek to move forward, even when we don't know what the future holds.

You can wallow in denial for a long time. Unlike shock, it will not pass on its own, but requires the courage to accept that which is scary and unknown. Face your future head-on, as hard as that may be, so you are best equipped to care for your child and your whole family. Denial may also reappear down the road. Don't be surprised if a change in condition brings about renewed feelings of denial. "He doesn't need that now! He's been stable and doing fine." "What do you mean the medicine is no longer working? We haven't noticed a change." Recognize those feelings for what they are: moments of grief amid an otherwise joyful life.

---

KEY TAKEAWAYS
- Denial is rooted in fear. Admit that you are scared of your child's diagnosis and the resulting uncertainty.

- Avoiding doctors, treatments, therapy appointments, and other special-needs parents makes it harder for you and your child to get the help and support you both need.
- Don't deny that you can have a happy family life, even with your child's diagnosis.
- Start talking with other special-needs parents to see how they manage their children's diagnoses. Speak honestly with them about your specific fears and concerns.
- When presented with a change in your child's condition, resist the urge to retreat into fear and denial rather than confront the new challenge head-on.

## Prayer to Saint George

You may not be literally fighting a dragon, but your child's diagnosis probably seems just as big and scary. We can't run and hide as much as we'd like. Remember Saint George and ask for his intercession as you work up the courage to fight this monster.

Faithful servant of God and invincible martyr, St. George; favored by God with the gift of faith, and inflamed with an ardent love of Christ, thou didst fight valiantly against the dragon of pride, falsehood, and deceit. Neither pain nor torture, sword nor death could part thee from the love of Christ. I fervently implore thee for the sake of this love to help me by thy intercession to overcome the temptations that surround me, and to bear bravely the trials that oppress me, so that I may patiently carry the cross which is placed upon me; and let neither distress nor difficulties separate me from the love of Our Lord Jesus Christ. Amen.*

---

*https://www.ewtn.com/catholicism/library/novena-in-honor-of-st-george-11864.

## Stage Three: Anger

Upon learning of my son's diagnosis, so many women's first response was to try to comfort me by sharing their own child's health struggles. They attempted to empathize by relating tales of peanut allergies, sprained ankles, and learning disabilities. Rather than helping, I often left these conversations angry and biting my tongue. I began to loathe every conversation with well-meaning people who approached me with the words, "I understand ..."

Often, I was put in the position of comforting and reassuring them that everything would be alright with their child rather than finding greater peace with my own situation. Tony and I started to feel resentment toward our friends and family who, in our eyes, were blessed with normal children and yet seemed hung up on trivial concerns that would in no way shorten their child's life or cause him or her pain or suffering down the road.

People offered us advice, or even product samples, of natural remedies. Others emailed or shared articles or newspaper cutouts with promising research for diseases that had nothing to do with SMA. I found myself explaining that vaccinations didn't cause SMA; it was a missing gene and not something I had control over.

It was also not uncommon for people to become emotional and break down and start crying as I told them about Fulton's diagnosis and robotically ticked off statistics about the disease. I tried to present a very strong front so I could help my friends and family members with their own emotions. Because they were struggling, I felt I couldn't open up to them about my own feelings, especially when, many times, I felt angry with them.

*How dare you cry about my son's diagnosis in front of me! I'm the one who needs a shoulder to cry on!*

*How dare you try to give me false hope and say he might still walk! Tell me it will be OK if he never walks!*

*How dare you compare your child's minor illness to my son's condition! Don't trivialize the severity of what we're facing!* No matter what someone said, I would feel angry. People didn't know how to relate to our situation, and I didn't know how to express my feelings of frustration at their lack of understanding, so I confided in others less and withdrew into myself. It seemed easier to bottle it up, feign strength and courage, and then lie awake at night worrying and crying.

Some people suggested we were special, spiritually blessed if you will, to be chosen to raise a child with special needs. Maybe they saw it as a compliment. I didn't see SMA as a blessing, but rather a curse upon my child and my family. I would never tell anyone they were lucky to get cancer, or lose a loved one suddenly to a heart attack, or that God thought they were special and that's why they suffered from infertility. I couldn't be grateful for this disease, and it seemed flippant to try to twist the situation in order to make myself feel good about it.

It sounded to me like they were telling me to thank God, when it was God himself whom I was most angry with. I blamed him for this awful disease and for every struggle, past, present or future, that would befall my son. If I was so "special," what did that make them? I'd rather not be special in the eyes of God if this was how he was going to treat me. And if I had a nickel for every time someone told me, "God doesn't give you more than you can handle!" with an ear-to-ear grin, I could have paid cash for Fulton's wheelchair. I was 110 percent sure I'd been given more than I could handle, and I didn't want my cares and concerns dismissed so flippantly with a clichéd saying.

I wish I would have been more honest with people at the time and told them how I was feeling. Because I'd refused to meet other SMA parents, I didn't have anyone to vent to who would understand and validate my feelings. I couldn't get the support I needed from my friends and family, so I struggled with my anger, and it interfered in my life in unexpected ways. It was a vicious cycle: Concerned people would ask how I was, I'd reluctantly share my concerns, they'd accidentally say something to anger me, I'd vow not to talk to people and bottle up my anger. But in becoming withdrawn, those who knew me would become more concerned and want to know how I was doing so they would ask ... and so on. I'm an extrovert, I love talking and socializing — and now it seemed I had lost most of the pleasure associated with these activities.

I didn't want to go out to social events or family gatherings because Fulton's diagnosis would often take center stage and lead to conversations that angered me.

Spiritually, emotionally, mentally, and even physically, I was being eaten up by anger. I could feel my pulse quicken, my face grow red, and my blood pressure rise during conversations between other people, and in my limited interactions with God. So I stopped praying and learned to bottle up all my anger. Unfortunately, it still came out. Usually more frequently when driving, when my kids were acting up, or when I was especially frustrated with some new aspect of Fulton's care. Almost anything could cause me to snap. I wasn't a fun person to be around anymore.

I moved quickly from shock to denial and then lingered in anger, and it coexisted with the next stage of bargaining, probably because I was prone to anger in everyday life already. Because I couldn't avoid being around people, I couldn't avoid the conversations that would inevitably upset me. It was the feeling of being the only person I knew who was carrying this load, a kind of special-needs isolation that finally moved me from anger into depression (with a brief stop at bargaining). If I was unhappy with the situation and had no one to help me process it, what was the point?

## What You Can Do: Alleviating Anger

It will be easy for you to recognize when you've reached the stage of anger. What will seem different from your experience of anger in the past is the particular things that trigger your anger now. Try to find out what is triggering your anger. Recognize that your response has less to do with what is triggering you, and more to do with your own complex emotions about your child's diagnosis.

Avoid situations that will make you unreasonably angry until you are able to respond appropriately. If you cannot avoid the triggering situations or people, be honest and tell them when their words or actions upset you, and that you cannot talk about or do the suggested things while you are still processing your child's diagnosis. Admit your struggles and ask for prayers for this specific intention.

Even when I was angry with God, I still found peace in the quiet of adoration. The stillness of the chapel could always calm my angry mind, even when I didn't know what to say to God in his presence. Go to confession more and confess your anger as much as possible, especially if you are bottling up your anger and directing it toward other people. Make time for quiet — whether outdoors, in a church, through prayer, mindfulness or meditation; allow yourself some space for peace.

Don't lash out at doctors, nurses, therapists, or anyone who works with your child. They aren't the cause of your child's diagnosis. There may be times when you need to advocate forcefully for your child, but in the first few months post-diagnosis, extend some grace to the medical professionals who are trying to help you, and seek a second opinion from another experienced special-needs parent or specialist if you have concerns. Take a friend with you to appointments to calmly advocate on your family's behalf if you don't feel you can keep a cool head for the near future.

Apologize to friends and family if anger shows up and directs itself at an innocent person. Don't beat yourself up if you find yourself flying off the handle more than usual. Anger is a normal step in the grieving process. It may seem like you have no time for yourself, but consider finding a physical outlet to release your anger: Running, walking, etc., may give you somewhere to direct your anger and frustration in a way that doesn't harm others.

It is easy to get stuck in the stage of anger. We feel justified in being angry with God, the world, the doctors — everyone, because our child has been given a devastating medical diagnosis. It's not fair. We want justice for our innocent child. We want to do something and change the outcome, but we can't, so we respond with anger. And the thing is, most of the world will agree with us — "it's not fair, it's terrible what happened to your child" — and they will justify your anger, even your anger at God. But we can't feed our anger and allow it to grow and fester, or bear a grudge toward God. Anger can put up a wall between us and not only God, but our loved ones as well.

You're right, your child's diagnosis isn't fair. But remind yourself that you are a better parent and caregiver when your actions are motivated by love, not anger.

---

## KEY TAKEAWAYS

- Try to recognize what triggers you to become unreasonably angry.
- Be honest with people about situations and conversations that make you angry, and why you need to avoid these things for the time being.
- Spend time alone, in silence, to help calm your nerves.
- Ask for forgiveness when you lash out, and seek out

confession more frequently.

- Take a knowledgeable friend or family member with you to medical appointments to advocate on your family's behalf if you are struggling to keep a cool head in such situations.
- Find a physical outlet to vent your anger: sports, exercise, etc.

## A Prayer for Release from Anger

Saint Jerome was known for having a bit of a temper. We can find solace in knowing that even the holiest of saints struggled with an emotion that may be overcoming us right now. This short prayer written by Saint Jerome can help us when we are lashing out at others from our woundedness.

O Lord, show Your mercy to me and gladden my heart. I am like the man on the way to Jericho who was overtaken by robbers, wounded and left for dead. O Good Samaritan, come to my aid. I am like the sheep that went astray. O Good Shepherd, seek me out and bring me home in accord with Your will. Let me dwell in Your house all the days of my life and praise You for ever and ever with those who are there. Amen.*

## Stage Four: Bargaining

I'd been to New York City a few times, but somehow never managed to make it inside St. Patrick's Cathedral. We learned shortly after naming our son Fulton that his namesake, Archbishop Fulton J. Sheen, lay (at that time) under the altar in a crypt at St. Patrick's. We had a few Fulton Sheen books and recordings in our home, plus a second-class relic on a holy card. After the diagno-

---

*https://www.learnreligions.com/prayer-of-saint-jerome-542709.

sis, we ratcheted up our devotion to this Servant of God, hoping his intercession would prove miraculous. A couple of months post-diagnosis, Tony decided we needed to take things to the next level. Sure, we'd been good Catholics, but clearly God wanted more from us; why else hadn't our son already been healed by our prayers?

Tony started focusing all his energy on planning a pilgrimage to New York City to touch Fulton to the tomb of Archbishop Fulton J. Sheen. Tony couldn't imagine raising a child with special needs. If he thought about the future at all, it had to involve a cure, miraculous or medical. Since the medical community couldn't give us any hope at the time, we had our hearts set on divine intervention. Tony tried to make a deal with God: "We'll do this big pilgrimage with all our kids, and lots of people from the parish, and then Fulton will get cured. OK, Lord?"

I kept my Protestant family in the dark about the trip until the last minute because I was afraid they'd think such a trip was wishful thinking, and I didn't want discouragement. I wanted to pull out all the Catholic stops when it came to my son, and I didn't want anyone dismissing the traditions and practices I was clinging to for dear life. I'd tried making deals with God in the past and fallen through on my promises, so I was perhaps more guarded than Tony. I wanted so desperately to be worthy of a miracle, and I guess I felt like I wasn't.

We rented a coach bus and packed it with people from our parish. Other families drove themselves up in vans. I tried to create a video that explained SMA to those on the bus. I knew people had questions, and outside of close friends, not everyone who came along understood what we were facing. I didn't want to give a speech, but when the bus's DVD player didn't work, I answered questions from a few people, controlling my own emotions as one woman finally understood the severity of Fulton's diagnosis and started to cry.

Our parish priest made arrangements to get me, Tony, and Fulton down into the crypt under the altar, which was usually off-limits to tourists. Our large group full of young families walked through the imposing St. Patrick's Cathedral, decked out in scaffolding from ongoing renovations. I snapped pictures of the side altars, while our older children explored the sanctuary.

I wondered what a miracle would look like if we got it. I tried to picture Fulton rising up and walking like the lame man healed by Peter and John. Would we all leap and sing for joy? I tried to tell God we would sing his praises and be the best Catholics ever if we could just get this one little thing.

When our group gathered behind the high altar and we went into the crypt, we saw a nun praying there. Our priest interrupted her rosary to ask her to pray for our family and our son. We put Fulton up against the wall with Sheen's stone. I snapped a picture of Tony smiling; Fulton was not quite sure what all this business was about.

We left the crypt and moved to the Eucharistic chapel and prayed with our tour group. As we left the cathedral, we stopped in the gift shop, and then walked around Rockefeller Center. There was no ray of light, no appearance of angels; by all accounts it was a normal, sunny, fall afternoon in New York.

We toured another church, loaded the bus, and went home. There was the palatable feeling of at least we had done something, but we were not granted our miracle. Afterward, Tony never spoke about the subject, except to always dismiss the possibility. He wouldn't allow his hopes to ever get that high again.

I wondered how God decides who gets miracles and who doesn't. I knew enough about the Faith to know he could bring good from Fulton's illness, but I'd hoped he would use a miraculous cure to make his point instead. Why not our family? What else could we do? What hadn't we done right? Weren't we open to life? Hadn't we been good Catholics? Why couldn't we get a miracle or, at the very least, find peace with our state in life?

Maybe there was just one more prayer or novena we needed to say, or perhaps another shrine we needed to visit. We wanted GPS-precise directions to a miracle, but that's not how God works.

If we couldn't negotiate with God, maybe we could defy science. Perhaps with more physical and occupational therapy, healthier food, and the latest therapy equipment we could realize fantastic, never-before-seen gains in a child with SMA! If we put in more time and effort we should be guaranteed something amazing; it was only fair. How could we give and give and give, and seemingly get nothing in return?

Without a miracle, it was easy to move from bargaining into depression. I developed a despairing resignation to the fact that God wasn't listening to our prayers, and we were obviously on our own to figure out life with a child who has special needs.

## What You Can Do: Ending the Bargaining

Bargaining with God is an argument we can't win. We can't approach our heavenly Father as if we're in hostage negotiations. We *can* counteract bargaining with trust. Rather than making one-sided promises and agreements with only our interests in mind, it helps to remember the wonderful things that have come from trustful surrender to God's plan. When we trust in the value of a product, we don't try to haggle or bicker over the price. We recognize its worth. We are willing to pay a fair price.

Your child has worth and value you don't recognize yet, but God does. He does not see your child as imperfect or flawed, and he wants you to see your child as he does. He hears your prayers and pleas, and rather than giving you what you're asking for right now, he's asking for your trust. You don't need to go on pilgrimages, wear sackcloth, fast for weeks on end, or upend your life with new spiritual practices and mortifications. God will certainly take all your good works and use them for your benefit, but that doesn't necessarily mean the miraculous cure of your child.

Untangle your feelings of your own shortcomings and failures as a Catholic, or human being, from your child's diagnosis. Realize your child's future health is not determined by how good of a person you are. "Then he said to them, 'My soul is very sorrowful, even to death; remain here, and watch with me.' And going a little farther he fell on his face and prayed, 'My Father, if it be possible, let this chalice pass from me; nevertheless, not as I will, but as thou will'" (Mt 26:38–39). It is OK to ask God to let this chalice pass. But if it does not, we must be willing, like Christ, to ascend our own Calvary, trusting in a greater glory to come. You may be willing to pay any price to regain a "normal" child, while within your grasp is loving and enjoying the child you have.

---

## KEY TAKEAWAYS

- God sees the value in your child just as he or she is right now.
- Your child, and family, can be happy without a cure, divine or medical.
- Your child does not have a disability because of some parental spiritual shortcoming. Therefore, your child's health is not dependent on your spiritual practices.

### Prayer for Trust in Jesus
Rather than continuing to bargain with God, step back and pray for trust. Even as the big picture eludes you, try to trust that God knows the good that can come from this situation.

O Christ Jesus, when all is darkness and we feel our weakness and helplessness, give us the sense of Your presence, Your love, and Your strength. Help us to have perfect trust in Your protecting love and strengthening power, so that nothing may frighten or worry us, for, living close to You, we shall see Your hand, Your purpose, Your will through all things. Amen.*

## Stage Five: Depression

In the early fall of 2009, Tony and I were finally getting an evening out sans kids at a parish event. Everyone around me was laughing, drinking beer, and swaying along to the loud polka music. The smell of bratwurst and sauerkraut hung in the air, and children in lederhosen ran haphazardly through the church hall. Our table of friends talked loudly and clinked steins. It was our parish's first Oktoberfest, and by all accounts it was a smashing success. I nibbled at my food and sipped my Riesling. I drifted in and out of conversations, distracted by my own thoughts rather than the blaring accordion. My husband and I had bought tickets as soon as they went on sale, expecting to be cheered up and to enjoy a bit of adult fun together for the first time in months. We had started attending a local Oktoberfest in our hometown back when we were in college. As our family grew, we traveled hours to attend the festival and tried to instill in our kids a love of bratwurst, lederhosen, polkas, and anything Bavarian. After tucking our kids into bed at their grandparents', we would go back out, meet friends, and sing loudly while dancing around the floor. We were thrilled when plans for a similar festival closer to home began to take shape in early 2009, but so much had changed for us since then that I wasn't surprised to find I wasn't enjoying myself.

---

*https://www.xavier.edu/jesuitresource/online-resources/prayer-index/ignatian-prayers.

"I can't keep sitting here pretending to have fun," I finally said to him, already feeling a lump in my throat. "I need to go sit alone in the chapel for a bit." Tony's face sank as he realized this rare date night was not the respite we had hoped it would be. "OK," he said. "Let me know when you want to leave."

I quickly walked from the church hall to the chapel. The lights were off and only the sanctuary lamp burned overhead. I sank down in a pew directly facing the statue of Our Lady, illuminated by a single spotlight. I exhaled deeply and began to cry. Soon my cries became deep, body-wracking sobs. I held my head in my hands and gasped for breath.

I had cried so much before this night, I was amazed I still had so much sadness and hopelessness left inside of me. I was glad everyone was too distracted by the music and alcohol to hear my sobs fill the empty chapel.

Despite almost four months having passed since Fulton's diagnosis, I was still devastated and still unable to be happy and find joy in my family, my friends, or even an Oktoberfest.

I spent my days tending to the needs of my young family of four kids, ages six and under. I tried to homeschool, keep on top of the laundry, and feed my children, while simultaneously making and attending numerous new doctor visits, arranging and assisting at in-home therapy sessions, and filling out paperwork for prospective drug trials. I was busy, and I tried to stay busy so as to not have time to stop and think.

Since our failed attempt at a miracle, every conversation between my husband and I was heavy, dark, and reflected our hopelessness. Instead of sitting together sipping coffee in the morning and discussing current events or our favorite reads, we simply sat and stared into our mugs ruminating, always next to each other but miles away in thought. We couldn't and wouldn't talk about a future that seemed scary.

As I moved away from anger and bargaining, even conversations with friends took on a more pessimistic slant. A couple of weeks before the Octoberfest, as a friend prepared to leave my house after a playdate between our children, my eyes filled with tears and I suddenly blurted out, "I just realized, he'll never be an altar boy!"

She tried to console me. "Maybe he will. Maybe they could modify —"

I cut her off. "He won't be an altar boy. He'll never be a priest." The enormity of those thoughts caught in my throat and I pulled myself together long enough to see her out the door, knowing her sons would all be on the altar helping Father within a few years. Now everything people said made me sad, and all I saw were the dire predictions and missed opportunities.

Perhaps my older son would never become a priest, or a professional football player, or a fighter pilot, but there was still a chance. Because these occupations were definitely out of reach for Fulton, I mourned the loss of these possibilities, as far-fetched as they were for any child. I tried to use dark humor to stop myself from upsetting other people or revealing how much I was hurting.

As I sat in the church for the rest of the Oktoberfest crying myself out to the point of exhaustion, I poured all that bottled-up pain at Mary's feet. No one could understand the pain in my heart except a woman who had watched her innocent son be scourged and hung on a cross to die. That was the only fate worse than spinal muscular atrophy that I could imagine happening to my child. I took comfort in knowing that at least one person understood my pain completely, but I wondered how I was supposed to recover from this grief when I was not perfect like Mary. Rationally, I understood my Catholic Faith and that God was with me during this struggle. I hadn't been abandoned and he hadn't given my son this diagnosis as a punishment or test.

But for the first time, I felt my deep faith could not transcend my deep pain. I had been talking the talk, but now I couldn't walk the walk. I couldn't even get up off the ground. I stopped praying unless it was in anger, or in sobs, or to question. I went through the motions of my faith — attending Mass, going to confession, instructing our children in our daily prayers — as if I was moving on autopilot. My mind was always elsewhere. Consequently, I felt like a bad Catholic. Here I was, where the rubber met the road, and I wasn't patient with the Lord like Job, or picking up my cross and joyfully skipping down the path to heaven.

Why couldn't I find peace? Why did I not find comfort and solace in the one thing, the most important thing, the truth of which motivated us to even have these four kids? Through all the previous stages of grief, I tried to maintain the outward appearance of a faithful Catholic, but my actions were superficial and could barely mask the despair that was eating away my faith.

After an hour in the chapel, when I finally stopped crying, I returned to the Oktoberfest celebration. I went to Tony and quietly told him it was time to leave. I knew that I was mentally, physically, and spiritually at rock bottom.

Reflecting on it now, I can still remember exactly how it felt; my chest tightens instinctively and my eyes begin to burn. My life overwhelmed me. I couldn't imagine carrying that load of grief around with me every day for the rest of my life. It was too much.

My oldest son, Byron, had a birthday party around the same time and a few moms helped me organize an afternoon of games and food for our pack of rowdy boys. One of the moms snapped pictures throughout the party and emailed them to me. As I viewed them later that night, a smiling picture of Byron and me filled the browser. There was a big cake between us, and you could tell he was eager to get to the cutting and consuming part of the party. I stared at my smiling face and remember thinking how amazing it was I could look so happy and glowing on the outside (it was a very flattering picture) and feel so horrible on the inside. I almost couldn't look at or enjoy that photo because my expression seemed like such a lie. I wasn't really having a fun afternoon as much as I wanted to for my oldest son's sake. The smile I wore in that photo and all the rest was fake. I saw how I was faking so much on a regular basis just to keep the status quo at home. It was all a charade.

I had a friend tell me that one day I would be happy again, but that seemed impossible. How could I ever be happy when Fulton had this awful disease? I didn't want to die, I wanted to raise my family. But living this way, devoid of joy forever, horrified me. The immensity of the darkness hanging over me was smothering.

When that party and a long-awaited Oktoberfest failed to raise my spirits, I knew I needed help. I recognized that I was depressed and even despairing, and that without a change, my children and marriage would be negatively affected.

## What You Can Do: Managing Depression

The depression that comes after the diagnosis of a child will last as long as we let it. If you cannot pull yourself out of depression, you will need to seek professional help to get your life back on track.

This is the last stage of grief. Like anger and denial, it may blend into other stages, but it represents the last major hurdle to taking control of your grief and achieving acceptance. As you recognize signs of depression, be forgiving of yourself. Remind yourself that the emotions you're experiencing (sadness, emptiness, etc.) are a normal part of grief and depression. You are not a failure as a Catholic, as a parent, or as a human being. God has walked with you through this grieving process every step of the way and he wants to take away the pain you're feeling. "For I, the LORD your God, / hold your right hand; / it is I who say to you,

"Fear not, / I will help you" (Is 41:13).

Now is when we need to choose not to allow our fallen human nature to dictate that we stay stuck in patterns of denial, anger, or depression. Some of us will only be able to do that with professional help, and that is OK. You are allowed to accept help in all forms to overcome the big emotions your child's diagnosis stirred up. Get help, and take care of yourself through the process. Don't let basic self-care fall to the wayside. Not sleeping, eating, or practicing basic hygiene is a sign you need professional help. Your journey through depression will not match anyone else's, probably not even your spouse's. Allow each other to process your feelings, and move through these stages in your own unique ways. Be as encouraging to one another as you can, but understand you may need outside support from friends, family, or professionals if you're both struggling. If your spouse chooses to stay stuck in depression, or any other stage of grief, for the sake of your own health and the well-being of your family, you must choose to take care of yourself and not allow his or her feelings to negatively impact your parenting and caregiving. Also encourage, pray for, love, and support your spouse, but know that until they are ready to move forward on the journey to acceptance, they will remain stuck where they are. Consider marital counseling if the clash of emotions is disrupting family life.

---

## KEY TAKEAWAYS

- Depression will last as long we let it.
- Sadness and depression are a normal part of the grieving process, and they represent the last stage before acceptance.
- You may need professional help to overcome depression, and that is OK.
- Your spouse may experience depression differently

from you. Encourage each other as you are able, but recognize the need for help outside one another.

- You cannot force someone to not be depressed.
- Focus on helping yourself, so you can continue to support a struggling spouse, while also being the best parent and caregiver to your other children.

### Prayer to Saint Dymphna

Grief has put us through the wringer, and now we feel at our lowest, physically, mentally, and spiritually. However, God has not abandoned us, and as hard as it may be for us to pray at times, we can still turn to him and ask for the intercession of his saints, to help us overcome this last hurdle of depression.

O God, we humbly beseech You through Your servant, St. Dymphna, who sealed with her blood the love she bore You, to grant relief to those who suffer from mental afflictions and nervous disorders, especially for help in overcoming the depression I feel related to my child's diagnosis.

Saint Dymphna, helper of the mentally afflicted, pray for us.

Saint Dymphna, comforter of the despondent, pray for us.

Saint Dymphna, renowned for many miracles, please hear my plea. Amen.

Glory be to the Father, and to the Son, and to the Holy Spirit, as it was in the beginning, is now, and ever shall be, world without end. Amen.*

---

*Hope & Healing: St. Dymphna Novena* from Diocese of Orange Office of Pastoral Care for Families of All Stages. https://www.rcbo.org/resource/mental-health-2/.

## Stage Six: Acceptance

A few days later, I stood staring at the religious bookshelf at my local library, anxious for some guidance, when I came across *Arise from Darkness* by Father Benedict Groeschel. The title accurately stated exactly what I was looking for — a way to rise out of my despair. Later that day, as Fulton lay on the floor on a tumbling mat, allowing an early intervention therapist to move his legs, I sat in a rocking chair by the woodstove, misty eyed. Father Groeschel's words finally started to crack through the depression and sadness I'd allowed to consume my soul:

> When we are knocked down and defeated by life ... that is when we can pick up the Cross and wave it at grief, sadness and death. To boast in the Cross, it seems to me, is an almost fierce gesture when we confront all that would defeat us and say: "Look at the Cross, all of you, and know that I shall not be overcome, because the Lord of Life is with me, and in me, and he will go with me even through the valley of the shadow of death."

I didn't immediately lay down the book after a couple of days of nonstop reading and feel 100 percent better, but Father Groeschel's words helped me find the humility to accept our situation without a miracle or divine explanation from God. I acknowledged that I couldn't control the situation, and I couldn't demand a cure or answers, but I could choose to be OK and love my son anyway.

The idea that I could "confront all that would defeat" me, and refuse to be overcome, helped me to see how I was allowing Fulton's diagnosis and the ensuing stages of grief to beat me down and have power over me. I realized I wanted to fight back; I wanted control of my life again. I couldn't change the fact that Fulton had SMA, but I wasn't completely powerless or a helpless victim. We can pick up our crosses and wave them at grief, and I was finally ready to do that.

Parents facing a devastating medical diagnosis or traumatic event need to acknowledge the stages of grief and admit it's not a failure of their faith to feel a certain way. We expect a certain type of life for our child, and from a young age we imagine them hitting certain milestones. To trade those dreams for an uncertain, and scary, future is a form of death. But as Christians, we acknowledge that no death is final. From the crucifixion, we received the Resurrection and everlasting life. From whatever cross God puts in front of our children and families, he can bring something good in this life and the next. Acceptance means having faith that God will bring good from your child's diagnosis.

Acceptance means you see the value in your child outside his ability to walk, talk, hold down a job, raise a family, or even survive outside the womb for more than a few hours. Acceptance means knowing God wanted your child to be here, and for you to be her parent. Acceptance means you understand your child has a purpose and mission in his life. Acceptance means knowing that while your child may never learn on grade level, gain fame, or hold a prestigious job, she can never be denied the kingdom of heaven.

However, acceptance isn't easy. Many special-needs parents stay trapped in the anger, bargaining, or depressive states of grief. Some parents only accept their child's diagnosis as a burden on themselves and their family. The disease is something only to be hated or healed; it can never be the cause of anything good. They can only see their child in terms of her limitations, her suffering, and her missed opportunities. They are blind to all the love and potential their children do have, even if they are medically fragile, nonverbal, or here only a short time this side of heaven.

When we view our child's disability through our own fears, anger, grief, and frustration, it's easy to see our children as victims and to feel hopeless. We see everything they can't do or won't live to see, and we miss all the happiness that's actually present. But our children are not burdens or hardships to be endured. They are gifts from a loving God to be loved and enjoyed so long as we are blessed to have them with us. That is the truth acceptance brings.

Because I went through all the normal stages of grief, I felt I wasn't a good Catholic, or good parent. I thought I should have been able to just accept circumstances and be patient with the Lord like Job. But in hindsight, I could clearly see how I moved through shock, denial, anger, bargaining, and finally depression. I recognized that holding on to any stage would no longer serve any useful purpose in my life. In fact, it could only serve to negatively affect my relationship with my children and husband. I learned that it was me, not God, who was dragging out the stages of grief. Grief is an ongoing struggle in many ways, but choosing acceptance yields benefits far greater than allowing yourself to sink further into sadness or anger. Choosing to stay angry or depressed may seem like the path of least resistance, and many people may not question if you do exactly that. But there is so much to gain and nothing to lose by embracing acceptance.

When I finally allowed myself to accept Fulton's diagnosis, I wasn't saying everything was fine. I was a completely different person. Our family would never be the same, or like any other family I knew. I would still have days when I got angry or depressed, but I could now have good days without feeling guilty for being happy. I could see everything my son was doing, rather than what he wasn't.

In many ways, acceptance for me became the practice of mirroring the way my older three children behaved. They simply saw nothing wrong with their brother, and happily worked harder to include him in their play. They didn't get sad when he couldn't do things. They loved him exactly as he was. Sometimes they got frustrated because I spent so much time with Fulton, or it seemed to them he was getting all sorts of fancy new stuff (actually medical equipment) when it wasn't even his birthday or Christmas. But attention-seeking and jealousy over gifts were parenting problems I tackled before SMA. Fulton's diagnosis didn't negatively impact my children, and I realized it didn't need to harm me either.

Christ tells us to have faith like little children, but why? As an adult whose life was upended by a medical diagnosis, I see how hard it is to maintain that trust and hope in God's divine providence. I would rather sit alone with my dusty prayerbook and read than have to joyfully accept my cross without question. It is harder for me to assume the best outcome, to keep hope that miracles (medical or divine) do happen. It is harder for me with all my "valuable life experience" to blindly accept that God always knows what's best. And yet, *that is my children.* That is most children. Untainted by cynicism, unburdened by despair, my children want to see the silver lining and can find it in the most troubling of circumstances. They refuse to give up hope, and will hold on to it long after I believe all is lost and that I have been forsaken.

I learned to look to my children for the example of how I should be. While my example is supposed to lay the groundwork for their future spiritual well-being, their example led me out of grief in all its stages and back to a simpler faith. They believe without question, without reserve, without hesitation. Reaching acceptance meant I was starting to break down my resistance to God's grace; the barriers of anger, despair, and pride that I allowed myself to construct. My children became my motivation to do better and my blueprint to follow.

My faith suffered after Fulton's diagnosis, not because God had done something wrong, but because I was not willing to commit myself to his plan for my life once I realized it did not look the way I wanted it to be. Acceptance helped me start to rebuild and renew my faith because I was willing to trust God again and not just plod through life, but love my life because everything in it was a gift from him. We are all called to be joyfully obedient to God's will in our lives, even when it's scary, heartbreaking, uncomfortable, and looks completely different from what we pictured our life to be. It means realizing that God calls us to do hard things that will require us to sacrifice and die a little to ourselves daily.

I had to work through the stages of grief because Fulton's life would not look as I imagined, and I needed to come to terms with that loss. But with acceptance, I came to realize that the life we did have in front of us, as new and uncertain as it seemed, could still be a life of joy. Life will be OK. Our family's life will be OK. Even if it's sometimes hard and messy, it will be OK, and more often than not, better than OK. It will be better than the safe, confined life to which we often try to constrain ourselves. Fear of the uncertain often limits us from experiencing greater love than we can imagine. There is joy and freedom in trusting God and allowing him to improve you and your family by your joyful surrender and acceptance.

## What You Can Do: Reaching Acceptance

Acceptance is a choice you make to leave the grieving process behind. There will still be tough times ahead. However, with acceptance, the emotions you wrestled with during the grieving process (denial/fear, bargaining, anger, depression) no longer determine how you tackle difficulties. You can make decisions from a place of love with a peace of mind not consumed with fear, sadness, or anger. You can advocate and fight for a cure or new, innovative treatments, or pray for a miracle, but be happy with your child as he is right now. If you are lucky, you will start to see the beauty of life through his eyes, and learn from his perspective rather than your own. If you have other children, look to see how they interact with their special-needs sibling. Do they model unconditional love and acceptance that you can learn from?

If you've struggled with your faith during the grieving process, hopefully now you can begin to rebuild trust in God's plan for your family, even without knowing or understanding all the whys. If you fell away from attending Mass and the sacraments, or stopped praying and practicing your faith, now is the time to ease back in. Go to confession and admit your struggles, past and present. Attend Mass with a contrite heart and admit to God that you're doing the best you can. Look up saints related to your child's diagnosis and create a family litany of saints to call upon when you're tempted to return to anger, denial, or grief.

If you continued to practice your faith, but were only going through the motions as my husband and I did, make the effort to reengage with your faith through increased participation and attention at Mass, and a more mindful attempt at prayers and regular devotions. Pick up a spiritual classic, or spend more time meditating on Scripture, to help reorient and reinvigorate your faith. Improving your faith may not lead to a miraculous cure, but you will see how it leads to the graces you need to thrive as the parent of a child with special needs.

---

## KEY TAKEAWAYS

- Acceptance means you now accept the reality of your child's diagnosis, and no longer need to cope with that reality through denial, bargaining, anger, or depression.
- Moving through the stages of grief is a normal healing process, but choosing to stay stuck in any one stage rather than moving into acceptance can prevent

you from enjoying your child and your family life.
- Don't let grief define your life as a special-needs parent.
- Life with a child who has special needs will be different than the life you envisioned for your child pre-diagnosis, but it can still be a good life.
- Put forth a renewed effort into practicing your faith. Meditate upon having childlike faith and humility.

## Prayer of Abandonment, by Blessed Charles de Foucauld

Moving into the stage of acceptance may not feel easy at times. Recite this brief prayer to help you surrender yourself with love to God's plan.

Father,
I abandon myself into your hands;
    do with me what you will.
    Whatever you may do, I thank you:
    I am ready for all, I accept all.

Let only your will be done in me,
    and in all your creatures —
    I wish no more than this, O Lord.

Into your hands I commend my soul;
    I offer it to you with all the love of my heart,
    for I love you, Lord, and so need to give myself,
      to surrender myself into your hands without reserve,
    and with boundless confidence,
      for you are my Father.
Amen.[*]

---

[*] https://www.ewtn.com/catholicism/devotions/prayer-of-abandonment-361.

# 2

# Life Will Look Different, and That's OK

## *The Grace of Hope*

"I think you need to take a pregnancy test."

I ignored Tony's comment. I was in charge of a homeschool conference that was less than a month away, plus Addie's first holy Communion the week after that. I didn't have the mental space to think about being pregnant.

"I'm not taking a test," I finally snapped at him. "If I don't take the test, I can pretend I'm not pregnant."

We both already knew the answer. I'd never missed a period without being pregnant; the pregnancy test was just a formality I needed to undergo for the benefit of the doctors. But I pushed the idea of a new baby to the back of my mind for a bit longer and, I assume by a sheer force of will, avoided any morning sickness through the next few busy weeks.

When I finally took the test and confirmed the obvious, Tony and I had to face the fact that by the end of 2010 we were going to add one more to our family. This time, we knew there was a one in four chance the baby would have spinal muscular atrophy like Fulton.

Up to this point, I would have said, "I'm doing better!" Fulton was quickly approaching his second birthday, so we were almost a full year out from his diagnosis. I was five months out from reading *Arise from Darkness,* and I continued to try to "wave my cross at grief" daily. Fulton remained healthy this whole time and was doing well with all the therapy and new routines. Though I wouldn't have launched into an explanation of the stages of grief, I believed I'd made it to the point of acceptance. Unfortunately, a new pregnancy revealed I wasn't really at peace with God's plan, especially if it included another baby. And the thought of another child with SMA seemed unthinkable and downright scary. The fact that many family members and outsiders couldn't accept God's plan for our family didn't help, and when we finally announced the pregnancy, they got angry, stopped talking to us, or ignored my growing waistline all together. One family member unfriended me on Facebook immediately after learning the news, while another's response was to argue with me about contraception. Imagine being at a family gathering where no one offers you congratulations about your new baby, just looks of concern and admonishments to take better care of yourself.

Thankfully we had good friends who themselves understood all too well the challenges of Natural Family Planning, and supported us simply by acknowledging that, although it was a challenging situation for us, our announcement was one of joy, even if we struggled to see that ourselves at the time. There would be no baby shower or sprinkle, no gender-reveal party, no maternity photoshoot. There was none of the former joyful anticipation for myself, Tony, or many of our family members.

The pregnancy proved to be my toughest to date. My blood pressure skyrocketed out of control and I found myself on bedrest by the second trimester. Homeschooling took place in our king-sized bed, when it happened at all. Soon after, Tony was laid off from his job. We now faced the prospect of delivering and bringing a new baby home with no health insurance. Tony's parents had been living with us for more than a year in a small, extra room upstairs, and the number of people in my home often made me feel like I was living in a tenement. Sound carried between all the rooms and floors. We had only one shower, and our main living space was also the playroom and schoolroom. The boys' bedroom was adjacent to the living room, so nothing above a whisper was allowed once Byron and Fulton went to bed.

The cramped living quarters, a surprise high-risk pregnancy, and now Tony's lack of a job seemed like more than we could handle. After all, we had only just come to accept the challenges with Fulton's diagnosis. The future, more than ever, was a dark and scary uncertainty. The weak amount of acceptance we'd managed to build quickly came crashing down. Because many people were angry with us for allowing another pregnancy to happen, I had to smile and pretend I was doing fine even as the physical and mental strain took its toll on my health.

Finally, after all the doctor's efforts failed to control my blood pressure, I was induced on the feast of Our Lady of the Rosary and Teddy was delivered early in the morning on October 8, 2010, at 32 weeks. Within days, we had him tested for SMA.

• • •

I was sitting behind the privacy screen in the neonatal intensive care unit holding Teddy, who had just completed another successful feeding session, when I heard footsteps approach. The doctor peeked around the edge. As I looked up at her expression, I immediately knew what she was about to tell me. She placed her hand on my shoulder and simply said, "I'm sorry."

I looked away. I didn't want to hear the rest of what she needed to tell me. I quickly stood up, already starting to sob, and placed Teddy in his isolete, muttered something about needing to go home, and ran out of the hospital unable to control my tears. I wanted to escape from that place and the diagnosis so badly that I wouldn't even let her speak to me.

I didn't know how I could tell my husband. Would I be able to say the words, "The test came back and Teddy has spinal muscular atrophy," or would I simply collapse into a heap upon walking into the house?

I opened the back door to see my husband in the kitchen making a favorite snack of peanut butter spread on Reese's cups. As he looked at me through the glass, I saw him spit out his food, throw the remainder in the trash and start yelling, "No! No! No!"

My tears, the look of pain on my face before I even made it into the kitchen, had been enough to tell him what I'd learned at the NICU. All our prayers, hopes, and heartfelt desires could not change the fact that our newborn son had the same devastating disease as his older brother. To this day, Tony no longer eats peanut butter on Reese's cups.

If one child with special needs was more than what most people could handle, how were we to manage two children with a degenerative neuromuscular disease, while also raising three other children?

We'd been down this road before, but the second diagnosis was harder for both of us than the first. Rationally, we knew Teddy would be happy and his life would be a blessing even with SMA, but we were thrust back into a deep grief. We, along with many of our closest friends, had believed that Teddy would be the "consolation baby," the healthy son to "replace" our child with SMA. For months, well-meaning people told me God would never give us another child with SMA; God would make sure this baby would be healthy. Tony and I took that belief to heart so that, when presented with the exact opposite result, we just couldn't believe it. All our misplaced hopes and dreams were torn down.

For those who were angry at us for getting pregnant in the first place, this diagnosis was not a surprise at all; what could we have expected? We simply got what we deserved. I couldn't look for sympathy or support from many of the same people who had rushed to my side at the news of Fulton's diagnosis.

Within our own cramped home, the news was received quite differently. Tony's parents struggled with the news as we did, almost arguing with us over the results. "He's so healthy and strong for a preemie, how can he have SMA?" his mother cried.

But our oldest three kids surprised us more than anyone. Through red-rimmed eyes, we sat them down on our sofa, Fulton laying happily on the floor in front of them, and delivered the news. "Guys, we have to tell you something important. We just learned that baby Teddy will be like Fulton," trying to keep my composure. "He has the same condition, and he will never walk either."

It took only a split second for them to erupt into cheers and screams.

"Yay! Now there'll be two wheelchairs to crash around and chase!"

"Fulton! Teddy will have a wheelchair like you!"

And they celebrated this exciting announcement, while Tony and I stared in amazement at one another.

"Well that went much better than I expected," Tony remarked.

We thought our kids would mourn Teddy's diagnosis the

way we did, but since they didn't see anything wrong with Fulton, our announcement didn't signify that anything was wrong with Teddy. In fact, Edie later admitted that she just assumed Teddy would be like Fulton because she thought (at age two and a half) that all younger brothers needed wheelchairs.

We thought we knew a lot about SMA and what our future with Teddy would look like that first year — missed developmental milestones and tons of doctor appointments — but like our expected response from our children, we were wrong.

• • •

Tony and I stood next to the crib in our room, the mattress set to the highest height for newborns, as we thought about his future.

"I guess we won't have to lower this mattress for Teddy. He'll never pull himself up," I muttered out loud, giving voice to one of the many sad predictions I was mentally making in those first few days post-diagnosis.

But before long, we did need to lower the mattress because Teddy did sit up in bed and try pulling up. Long after the point where Fulton stopped progressing, Teddy continued to meet milestones, even when adjusted for his prematurity. As Fulton laid on a tumbling mat on the floor, Teddy sat next to him and happily stole Fulton's toys.

One day, as we sat on the sofa watching the boys, we realized Teddy was trying to crawl. I started placing items just out of reach and he scooted for them. Within a week, he was cruising around the floor. Soon after, he started to stand independently when placed against the couch or a step. He could even pull himself up on items lower than his chest.

Despite all the dire predictions, Teddy was not as weak as Fulton. In fact, for one whole year, we had by all appearances a typical, healthy baby. It was not the miracle we prayed for. It was not a cure. But Teddy's progress was an answer to prayers and the balm my soul needed to move to acceptance again.

Unlike me, our older children moved immediately into acceptance. There was never any anger or sadness — they had a baby brother! Teddy was always to be celebrated and spoiled, and it never occurred to them that he wasn't exactly the way he was supposed to be. They didn't have to work through any preconceived notions of what a normal child was supposed to do; Teddy just did what he did and that was enough. They had no expectations that things should be otherwise, so they couldn't fret over the what-ifs.

Once again, their innocence helped me in my own journey of learning to trust God's plan. Although not one to talk about his feelings, Tony admitted to finding his own peace and acceptance in coming home from his new job and simply watching the children all play happily together.

My children accepted that this was how our family was supposed to look, and so I too accepted that this family with five kids, eight and under, two of whom had a degenerative neuromuscular disorder, was the one I was meant to have. Even though we looked like no other family I'd ever known, everything would be OK.

We'd finally moved into the acceptance stage after a prolonged second trip through shock, denial, anger, and depression that lasted almost a year. (We skipped bargaining — I think we just assumed we wouldn't get a miracle, so why bother asking or negotiating for one?) I was laughing at my kids' silly antics, enjoying moments in our days, and finding things to be thankful for. Our days and weeks soon had a routine of therapy and early intervention visits. I came to find the strength I needed to do what needed to be done, day in, day out; and it wasn't the awful drudgery one imagines when first presented with the idea of special-needs parenting times two. My day was different than most, and hard at times, but it was not bad. It was as good and joyful as when I was raising three typical kids.

God was answering our prayers through small miracles, small joys — and in small steps, I came to see that he would help us through these earth-shattering diagnoses, not by huge Red Sea-parting works of grandeur, but with help through the everyday challenges. By taking it one day at a time, I could hope for the next day, and then the next, and before long the future seemed manageable. I could trust that even if something bad happened (again), God would see us through it — even if we were angry, scared, disappointed, or uncertain.

No planner, list, or instructional video was going to prepare me for every challenge that lay ahead, nor take every contingency into account. The future would hold more problems, but even though I couldn't stop the inevitable, I could learn to not be defeated by it the way I had been when we received the boys' diagnoses. I could focus on the good to come, even if it wasn't easily apparent, and the moments of joy, even if they were few and far between. Nothing has taught me how to trust in God more completely than having absolutely no control over a situation.

Grief continually threatened to creep back into my life and take over my day by shifting my focus to the boys' limitations, and the limitations the world places on disabled people. I could lose myself in those thoughts, begin to feel sorry for myself, and become angry with God again for placing our family in this situation.

Whenever those thoughts began invading my mind, I had to stop and really look at my children. Seeing the joy that Fulton and Teddy experienced in their lives helped me see that the only person feeling sad about their diagnosis was me. As I saw the relationships between them and their siblings grow, I realized that SMA was only going to negatively affect our lives as much as I let it. Just because our family looked different didn't mean we couldn't be happy. Just because my daily routine was more labor-intensive than most didn't mean I couldn't be happy. Living out my life with joy, and relying more steadfastly on God, healed the hurt I held in my heart. God's plan for my life included a lot of things I didn't think I wanted, but soon learned were some of the biggest joys of all.

## What You Can Do: Discovering Hope

Your new life is full of joy; if today you see joy and tomorrow you see joy, it's a safe bet that more joy lies down the road. While struggling with grief, it was probably impossible to feel anything but apprehension toward the future. But now, with acceptance and the recognition of joy, hope seems like a real possibility for the first time in a long while. "Be strong, and let your heart take courage, / all you who wait for the LORD!" (Ps 31:24).

No longer will you need to fake enjoyment, or don an artificial smile — you will actually start feeling happiness again. You may even start to catch yourself feeling the way you did before your child's diagnosis. This doesn't mean you don't recognize the severity of your child's condition, but that knowledge no longer robs you of joy. You will find you can talk about your child without becoming as emotional, and perhaps you'll be able to even focus a whole conversation on things completely outside his or her diagnosis. Your new life is different, and while special-needs parenting plays a large role in it, it's becoming more normal to you and less overwhelming. You will begin to recognize where God is answering your prayers, maybe not in the ways you expected or asked, but you catch glimpses of his plan and how it just might work out better for your family than you imagined. You can hope that, yes, some good might come out of this pain after all. Trusting God becomes easier and easier, and you can let go of the feeling that you need to control everything yourself. You can trust that if your child faces a new complication or secondary diagnosis, you will be able to handle it, because you've done the hard work and gotten this far already. You know you can do it again. That knowledge is powerful because it gives you hope that, no matter what, the future will be OK — and more than likely, better than OK.

Hope is a noun and a verb. It is not only the action of believing in a positive outcome. It is a specific desire on which we focus. Once you have reached acceptance, you will find yourself able to hope for a positive outcome for your child, regardless of their disability. You may not know what that positive outcome will be, as it will probably look different from what you expect for typical children, but the act of hoping is finally possible. When you make the fulfillment of God's plan for your child the thing you are hoping for most, that is when your acceptance is no longer contingent on your own dreams and experiences. It becomes a hope that springs from complete trust and faith in God's plan, now and far into the future. I found acceptance and hope after Fulton's diagnosis, but after Teddy's diagnosis, I needed to move from simply hoping for the best to realizing that our greater hope rested in Christ. My children's joy taught me that hope was possible, and brought me fully back to a state of acceptance. In the many years since then, when things didn't go our way, when there were pains and struggles, it has not been my vague hopes for the future or my children's innocent belief that pulled me through. It is because of a complete reliance on God, and a hope that finds peace in him through all things. A life following Christ as a special-needs parent will look ridiculously different than anyone else you know. You can accept it and find the joy in it each day when trust in God's plan is the hope to which you commit.

## KEY TAKEAWAYS

- Seeing the joy in today helps you see the joy in tomorrow.
- Life will take on a new normal, and you'll start to feel the way you did before your child's diagnosis.
- You will be able to trust God more as you see him answer your prayers in ways you may or may not have imagined.
- You will start to regain hope for your child's future.
- Even as new problems arise, you will learn that as your hopes for the future align more closely with God's plan, you will find peace and continued acceptance.

### Novena to Saint Jude Thaddeus

Saint Jude Thaddeus is known as the patron of hopeless causes, so if you find that despite discovering the joy in your life, you are still struggling to find hope, turn to him and ask for his intercession. The name Jude means "giver of joy," and so it seems especially fitting to turn to him when, despite your best efforts at acceptance, you might at times be overcome with worry, doubt, and lack of faith. Hopeless causes are ones we don't give up on, no matter how challenging and insurmountable they seem. Ask Saint Jude to help you regain the joy you had prior to your child's diagnosis. Ask him to help renew your trust in God so the future can seem less threatening and more hopeful again.

Most holy apostle, Saint Jude, faithful servant and friend of Jesus, the Church honors and invokes you universally as the patron of hope. Please intercede on my behalf. Make use of that particular privilege given to you to bring hope, comfort, and help where they are needed most. Come to my assistance in this great need that

I may receive the consolation and help of heaven as I work with my challenges, particularly (here make your request). I praise God with you and all the saints forever. I promise, blessed St. Jude, to be ever mindful of this great favor, to always honor you as my special and powerful patron, and to gratefully encourage devotion to you. Amen.*

Our Father ... Hail Mary ... Glory Be ...

---

*http://forms.shrineofstjude.org/site/PageServer?pagename=ssj_shrine_celebrate.

# 3

# Thankfulness in the New Normal

## *The Grace of Gratitude*

I feel like we coasted through Teddy's first year in a blur. We weren't sleeping. We were still often overwhelmed with the boys' care and schedule of appointments. I have some vague recollection of homeschooling my older children during that time, but I'm hard pressed to remember what we actually did for those 180 days. I can see now this is why Tony's parents were living with us — as stressful as it was at times, they provided constant comfort to the rest of our kids and helped mightily with meals and chores. When they finally moved out, they remained just down the street for many years, always ready to step in and help at a moment's notice.

In the months immediately following Teddy's first birthday, we started to watch his strength decline. It was hard at times to see him lose the ability to do what he once could, but it didn't destroy me the way I thought it would. I didn't relapse into grief, I accepted it, and celebrated everything he could still do. I found joy in Fulton maintaining his strength and finding ways to do big boy things in his own way.

My older children maintained close relationships with their brothers, and when I worried that perhaps I wasn't giving the older three the attention they needed, they reassured me by their eagerness to always help their brothers. When they sometimes complained or pouted about all of Fulton's new stuff or special visitors (medical equipment and therapists), I would remind them that Fulton needed these devices and special help to do things they could already do for themselves. Rather than resent or feel sorry for their brothers, they expanded their playful threesome to include both brothers however possible.

Nevertheless, I couldn't ignore that our homeschool was struggling. Because of the needs of the youngest two boys, the education of the older three often slid by the wayside, especially with Edie, who was so good at playing with the boys so I could get housework done. Tony's parents were always eager to help, but I didn't always need Grandma — I needed someone with medical expertise. We decided to look into nursing to free up more of my morning. I was thrilled when our insurance company agreed to give us seven hours of nursing care. Fulton only reluctantly agreed to let someone who wasn't me, Papa, or Grandma handle his care, but eventually he started to ask for his nurse instead of me. There was now always someone to get Fulton a drink or a dropped crayon, to reposition him or scratch his head. The nurses kept Fulton on a schedule and helped me to do the same. Often, Fulton and Teddy would sit together and play under the eyes of the nurse, and I could focus on homeschooling. There were still some complaints. I would still occasionally yell or maybe tears would emerge, but we started getting back on track and doing some of the fun games and activities I'd wanted to do, but never found time for amid the needs of the boys.

Fulton's schedule, my schedule, and the schedule of the rest of the family fell into place. We started our day with breakfast, prayers, and then schoolwork. I usually finished making sure the boys were ready for the day after the big kids finished their work. When the boys played, I checked work, helped with math, and tried to stay on top of the housework. We all ate lunch together, and by the afternoon, the older kids were free from schoolwork. Once chores were done, they could spend the rest of the day as they saw fit. The nurse left when Fulton went down for a nap in the afternoon. Even when Teddy no longer wanted to nap, Fulton always benefited from additional sleep, and the house was a bit quieter for a while.

When the witching hour of dinner prep appeared, I usually put on loud music in the kitchen to drown out the screams and tried to keep everyone busy with screens, books, or threats. By the time Tony came home I was spent. I tried to pass off as much responsibility as possible. Tony would grade the kids' Latin schoolwork, and after dinner would play the board or card games I never enjoyed. Finally, we gathered on the couches before bedtime for family prayers. The boys, and usually me, would be asleep soon after. The days were full, but having the extra set of hands during the day helped me find more time, and maybe even some more energy.

• • •

It's rare to find a mom of many with a complete baby book for each child, or any child after the first. I couldn't document cute milestones in a Hallmark album for my two youngest sons, or at least I didn't want to try. But during Teddy's first year, I did manage to update friends and family, and keep some future record, via notes and photo albums on Facebook. He was my first child to be fully documented from pregnancy announcement forward on social media.

I wasn't blind to the fact that people wanted updates on our unique family. We were quite possibly the only people they knew with two physically disabled children (or even one for that matter), and Facebook gave them a way to learn about special-needs parenting without seeming nosey or pestering me with questions.

My background is in writing, and I processed much of Fulton and Teddy's diagnoses through journaling, and a few depressing posts on an anonymous blog I ran that was supposed to be focused on homesteading and Catholic social justice.

Now I wanted to write and share more. Rather than brooding over my feelings, I decided to focus on the joyful, the happy, and all the good in my day. I wanted to take the funny status updates that showed my friends our life was not miserable and unthinkably hard, and expand on them. Old friends would say I was known for my quirky sense of humor and sarcasm, but I'd lost that part of myself while I worked through grief, twice. I didn't want to be known as the sad, frazzled mom of children with special needs. I didn't want my children remembering me as always angry and overwhelmed. So, on a whim, shortly after we were approved for nursing, when it seemed I might have a bit more free time on my plate, I started another blog called *This Ain't the Lyceum*.

At first I toyed with the idea of making it a serious "how to homeschool" blog, but when I checked out the competition, I realized I actually knew nothing about how to homeschool, and my lesson plans were downright ugly compared to the expertly designed floral masterpieces I saw online. I decided to have the anti-perfect homeschool, homemaking, Catholic mommy blog, thus the name poking fun at Socrates's school for learning. I decided I wouldn't just be real or honest; I would be ridiculous, funny, and purposely laugh at myself and how messy my schoolroom was, or how many coffee stains were on my bathrobe. By choosing to be silly, I forced myself to see my life through that lens, of a woman who wanted to tell a funny story. By spotlighting those quirky moments in our day, I couldn't help but see the laughter and the joy in each moment.

I'd always been one who liked to crack a joke, but there was nothing funny about SMA. As I started my blog, there still wasn't anything funny about it, but the description of our typical and chaotic family prayers was downright hysterical. So was writing about the crush I had on other homeschooling moms and their foolproof instructional methods. I would often sit at my computer in the early morning hours before anyone else was awake, laughing at my descriptions of our school day, my attempt to take everyone on a field trip, and ridiculous posts about my favorite possessions or latest outfit (which might have been fashioned out of an old sleeping bag). Writing these posts helped me to see how wonderful our life was, and how I was actually grateful for all of it, even though to many people my life was something to be pitied.

A part of me that had been slumbering awakened with this new outlet. I still had as much hard stuff to do as before, but I looked at my day and tried to see the good I could share, and where I could carve out some time for myself — a rare luxury. I was no longer "just" a homeschooling mom or a special-needs mom. I was a writer again!

I didn't write much about SMA in the beginning, and I didn't share much information about the boys, except to mention something about a wheelchair occasionally. I met other bloggers online and we bonded in the comment boxes over large family living, homeschooling concerns, and whether or not it was possible to be fashionable with snot or spit-up on every article of clothing one owned.

I gained a reputation for being funny and friendly, which is pretty much the exact opposite of who I'd been during the previous three years. I felt like I'd regained a part of myself. I was writing things I loved, and this outlet outside homeschooling made up for the fact that it wasn't easy to leave the house.

As I sat and typed out post after post, morning after morning, and read comment after comment between diaper changes, doctor appointments and sibling squabbles, I knew I'd finally reached the point where my life was as full of life and joy as it had been pre-diagnosis — because now I could go back and read the evidence. There was proof! The blog gave me funny stories to turn to on the hard days; or conversely, I could write about the hard days, and then come back and see how we'd overcome that particular struggle. When you're in the midst of caring for so many small, needy humans, it can be hard to look back and remember the good moments, but the blog saved all those moments for me.

One of the most memorable was when we lost the nursing I'd come to rely on so heavily. After only seven months, the insurance company realized there'd been an error. They'd approved our family for seven hours of overnight nursing. We could only use those hours when Fulton was asleep and hooked up to G-tube feeds and his BiPAP. The nursing agency had made a mistake by allowing us to use those hours during the day when the insurance company believed I didn't need the help.

I got the call delivering the news on a day I was pouring mimosas for my homeschooling mom friends. We were having an epic preschool playdate and it was my 34th birthday. When the phone rang showing the insurance company's number, I picked it up hoping the call would be quick. As the representative on the other end proceeded to tell me we'd be losing our nursing care, effective that week, I started pleading and crying. "What? How? Why? This week? But Fulton's regular nurse is away! You mean he loses care before she comes back?" A mom who stood next to me waiting for her mimosa overheard the conversation and immediately started filling my cup with more champagne. I hung up and asked all the other moms to step outside with the kids. I had more phone calls to make. Unfortunately, after many calls, apologies and — finally at the end of a fruitless week — goodbyes, we were done with nursing.

I took to my blog and vented and asked for prayers. People wanted to raise money, not understanding the large amount that would need to be raised to maintain the level of care we had long-term. For the next few weeks I scaled homeschooling back to the basics, assigning the kids only online math and language arts, while I tried to figure out a new way to get everything done, at least until we got a nurse back. But as weeks became months, I started thinking in terms of what to do if we never got nursing back.

Ultimately, I realized God didn't answer my prayers or the prayers of my readers by bringing nursing back. Instead, God helped me find a new peace and a new normal in my day. I shared this insight online, recording the initial lows and the new highs.

Saving it all on the blog helped me see the transition from panicked mom, to joyful, trusting mom again. I appreciated having a lasting document of the way God brought me through that situation and made me stronger from it, in a completely unexpected way.

• • •

Despite the strides I made in managing my time, the homeschooling, and the care of my children, I could never bring myself to be grateful for SMA. However, I was grateful that Fulton and Teddy had power wheelchairs to get around our house. I was grateful for the medical equipment that saved Fulton's life and kept him healthy. I was grateful to have two more happy sons to love and hold. I was grateful for the creative moments of play between my children. I didn't need to be reminded of the downside of SMA, but by being grateful for all the joyful parts of my day, I didn't spend all my time viewing SMA as a black pall that hung over everything. It became simply a nuisance to be avoided.

By sharing those moments online, I hoped other people would see the joy in our family too. The naysayers were wrong. Teddy wasn't a mistake, and SMA wasn't a punishment doled out on a helpless child by two careless parents or an angry God. Teddy and Fulton are blessings, and exactly the people God intends them to be. That I was chosen to be their mother is a blessing, not something to be pitied. I wanted to reach people who were angry at our fifth pregnancy, people who felt we got what we deserved when Teddy had SMA, people who balked at large families, strangers who thought Catholics who didn't contracept were crazy and backward.

I wanted our story out there to show those people that they were wrong. We weren't suffering with the consequences of bad decisions; we were living a life as full of joy as anyone else's, and possibly even thriving, because I'd finally learned to be grateful for the joy that was right in front of my face. Sharing the daily stories of my life showed me acceptance was the first step, but now I had embraced my life and could finally be thankful for it, disabilities and all.

## What You Can Do: Expressing Gratitude

You've reached the point of finding joy in your day, now remember to be thankful for it! It's so easy once the next tantrum or medical crisis emerges to forget those joyful moments. Work to make gratitude a new part of your daily routine. A quick prayer of thanks when something goes right can help you find the silver lining to almost any circumstance. When you're going through a particularly rough patch, ask God to help you find the moments to be thankful for, and pray for an increase in gratitude. Saint Paul reminded the Thessalonians to "Rejoice always, pray constantly, give thanks in all circumstances; for this is the will of God in Christ Jesus for you" (1 Thes 5:16–18).

When our life looks different from other families we know, it's easy to constantly focus on those differences and see them as negatives, and let them overshadow all the good in our day. It's worth the extra effort to seek out the joyful moments and make a point of offering thanksgiving to God. If you can document these blessings, all the better. Journaling, blogging, sketching, or snapping a photo to remind you of this newest joy will give you something to revisit in the future when maybe things aren't going as well. You can even consider using a dedicated gratitude journal or app for this purpose.

You are also providing a valuable example to your family of Saint Paul's exhortation. Your children may start picking up on the habit of being thankful, and it may help them overcome any habits of complaint, selfishness, or pessimism that may arise from having a medical diagnosis or living with a sibling who has a diagnosis. In a nutshell, if Mama (or Papa) is happy, everyone is happy!

It's easier to be optimistic, hopeful, and downright happy when you view life through the lens of gratitude. It changes your thinking from wondering or worrying how things "should be" to embracing how they are. When you find yourself complaining, stop and offer one prayer of thanks for every complaint. It won't be easy, especially at first, but in time you will enjoy finding things to be thankful for, and those moments will be the ones that define your day.

If anyone had a right to complain, it was Saint Paul. After being a successful Pharisee who gained a reputation for persecuting the followers of Christ, his conversion required that he be physically struck down and blinded. And that was only the beginning of his struggles! From imprisonment, shipwrecks, persecution to finally martyrdom, Saint Paul had every reason to be miserable, but by all accounts he wasn't. He continued to spread the Gospel despite hardship and, as we read above, encourage others to be joyful and give thanks as well!

## KEY TAKEAWAYS

- Don't just acknowledge the joy in your day, give thanks to God for it.
- Consider recording the things you are thankful for in a journal, blog, sketchbook, or photo album.
- Your continued practice of "giving thanks in all things" is a powerful example to your family.
- A focus on gratitude helps stop complaining.

### Prayer to Saint Paul the Apostle

Use this prayer to ask Saint Paul to help you find the joy and gratitude in each day.

O glorious Saint Paul, who from a persecutor of Christianity, didst become a most ardent Apostle of zeal; and who to make known the Savior Jesus Christ unto the ends of the world didst suffer with joy imprisonment, scourgings, stonings, shipwrecks and persecutions of every kind, and in the end didst shed thy blood to the last drop, obtain for us the grace to receive, as favors of the Divine mercy, infirmities, tribulations, and misfortunes of the present life, so that the vicissitudes of this our exile will not render us cold in the service of God, but will render us always more faithful and more fervent.

**V.** Pray for us, Saint Paul the Apostle,
**R.** That we may be made worthy of the promises of Christ. Amen.

Let us pray.

O God, Who hast taught the multitude of the Gentiles by the preaching of blessed Paul the Apostle: grant unto us, we beseech Thee, that we who keep his memory sacred, may feel the might of his intercession before Thee. Through Christ our Lord. Amen.*

---

*https://www.catholicculture.org/culture/liturgicalyear/prayers/view.cfm?id=1281.

# 4

# Count Your Crosses

*The Graces of Fortitude and Perseverance*

The cold had run its course through our whole family, taking down each man, woman, and child for days at a time, eating up the entire month of March in early 2011. While everyone else recovered, even five-month-old Teddy, Fulton struggled, weak and congested, long past the point when the other four were back to bouncing off the walls. He didn't want to eat or drink. In a last-ditch effort, my mother-in-law tried feeding him ice cream as he lay lethargic in a beanbag chair, anxious to pack calories into him and hopefully perk him up. We'd learned that kids with SMA have a tougher time with respiratory infections, but this was our first experience with a serious cold Fulton couldn't shake. I'd heard of things like cough assist machines and wondered if we should have one for times like this. We were hardly experts in the boys' condition yet, and since I'd resisted making friends in the SMA community, I didn't know who to ask for advice. Finally, as a fever appeared, we took him to the Children's Hospital of Philadelphia Emergency Department where we would be thrust into the deep end of caring for a medically fragile child.

We soon learned Fulton had a dangerously low blood oxygen level and pneumonia in one of his lungs. We were admitted and told to expect to be in-patient for several weeks. I was still nursing Teddy, and brought him along with me every morning. Tony would come over after work in the evenings and spend the night.

Tests revealed Fulton was aspirating thin liquids, meaning when he swallowed something like juice or milk, some of it dripped into his airway and collected in his lung, becoming an infection. We had to learn to place a feeding tube (or nasogastric [NG] tube) into his nose and down to his stomach to help him get enough calories, and we needed to thicken anything he wanted to drink. But once you've got juice mixed to the consistency of honey, is it any wonder he didn't want to drink it anymore?

I was introduced to the cough assist machine, which helps create the pressure needed for weak kids to have a good cough and clear their lungs. Fulton hated it, and often didn't cooperate, and then screamed as long suction tubes were stuck up his nose and down his throat to remove all the gunk he couldn't clear himself. He was placed on a BiPAP machine with oxygen and learned to sleep with a mask covering his face. The machine would force a little extra air into his lungs with each inhale. Respiratory therapists, nurses, and doctors were in and out of his room, constantly educating me on a whole side of SMA I'd been blissfully ignorant of until then.

When Fulton was finally discharged after "only" thirteen days, they sent a medical equipment company right over to drop off all our new equipment and explain everything to us. The downstairs bedroom became a mini hospital suite, and we learned to perform various medical tasks on our son. Although we were home, there was still a litany of things that needed to be done to help Fulton finish his recovery, and a slew of new follow-up appointments were scheduled.

SMA had come in and completely upheaved our life, changed it, and promised to barge back in again next cold and flu season. More steps were added to Fulton's care — more things I couldn't forget to do, more things to do in a day, and less time for me to sit down and relax for one moment. How was I going to find the time to do all this on top of homeschooling and caring for the other four kids? And how much longer until I had to do all this new stuff with Teddy?

Rather than resent all this additional work, I tried to view it as another way of serving my son and loving him. Even when it was uncomfortable for Fulton to have a new tube placed down his nose, or breathing treatments disrupted his playtime, I tried to remain calm and remember that sometimes what we need for our health, both physically and spiritually, doesn't feel good. It wasn't easy. I got angry, I cried, and I had embarrassingly little patience. In usual fashion, I created lists and plans on how to make all these new items fit neatly into our days, with mixed results of success.

It was not in lists that I found peace, but in knowing this situation was in God's hands, not mine. I only had so much control over Fulton health, the competence of the medical staff, and my own ability to remember everything that everyone needed at any given moment. I had to trust that as long as I continued the work laid in front of me, God would handle the rest. I couldn't live in the past, beating myself up for what I did or didn't do, and wondering if that was why Fulton got sick. I couldn't perfectly plan everything so that he'd never get sick again.

Ultimately that was not Fulton's last hospital stay. We became quite familiar with planned and unplanned in-patient visits. Trips to the hospital are always a disruption, but we learned to accept the intrusion and thank God for modern medicine rather than curse at the boredom, monotony, and separation from one another.

Moving through our days, whether it be at home or in a hospital, with a typically developing child who's having a tantrum, or a child with special needs who requires a breathing treatment, we can choose to either offer up our struggles and see them as our Little Way like St. Thérèse of Lisieux, or view them with disdain and only as a distraction from our preferred path in life. Just like a body builder gains strength by lifting weights constantly, I became stronger as I persevered through the things I didn't understand, and offered up the worry and drudgery rather than complaining and pitying myself.

Hospital stays, illness, and surgery are not happy times. They remind you all too clearly of your child's weaknesses and the reality of their diagnosis. I can be grateful in these times, but if my child is suffering, there is little joy. These dark times require fortitude — an inner strength that can only come through trusting in God, no matter what. It's why, when I'm rejecting God and his grace, these times are understandably harder.

I have heard more times than I care to remember the saying, "God doesn't give you more than you can handle." People have meant it to mean I'm special, I'm a superhero, and that I can do all things. Often in the same conversation I hear the phrase, "I could never do what you do." So people think that God hasn't burdened me, but if the same tasks fell to them, they'd be completely incapable of doing them.

I constantly feel like I've been given more than I can handle and that I can't do all that's being asked of me. Does that make me a bad Catholic? Am I just not holy enough to handle everything with a smile? No. What I've learned is that I'm not being asked to do anything by myself; when I feel like I must, that's pride. God wants me to sacrifice and work hard, but he wants me to find rest and comfort in him and, as I'll go into later, accept help from others. "Come to me, all who labor and are heavy laden, and I will give you rest" (Mt 11:28). Not only will Our Lord give me the grace I need, I will be refreshed by it. I will come away as one from an oasis, ready to journey forward.

This life is not one that needs to be slogged through with gritted teeth.

Practicing the virtues of fortitude and perseverance doesn't mean I'm the sole gold medal athlete at the Special Parenting Olympics; it's just two forms of virtue, strengthened by grace, that help me through the challenging times — like devouring a protein bar in the middle of a marathon. It's holy protein.

In his papal election address, Pope Benedict XVI said, "The fact that the Lord knows how to work and to act even with inadequate instruments comforts me, and above all I entrust myself to your prayers. Let us move forward in the joy of the Risen Lord, confident of his unfailing help. The Lord will help us and Mary, his Most Holy Mother, will be on our side."*

Sitting on the throne of Saint Peter versus raising a child with special needs are two completely different things, but that feeling of being overwhelmed, of being saddled with a task too great, is very similar. Nevertheless, God knew what he was doing when he blessed us with this work, so choosing to persevere means we choose to love the task at hand, whether it's sitting bedside in the hospital, or reading *Hop on Pop* for the nine millionth time, rather than complain about it. If you realize you missed administering a dose of medicine, or fed your child something you shouldn't have, don't beat yourself up and consider yourself a failure. Persevere by accepting your mistake and then immediately working to fix it, realizing this mistake doesn't determine your worth as a parent or child of God.

---

*http://www.vatican.va/content/benedict-xvi/en/speeches/2005/april/documents/hf_ben-xvi_spe_20050419_first-speech.html.

When we keep our eyes on the big picture, on God's unending love and support and blessings and joys he's given us in our present circumstances, we can persevere, even when illness or problems arise.

We excel in fortitude when we fight for the good life we know our children and families deserve, despite discrimination, inaccessibility, and a society increasingly unable to see the value in each human life. We are patient and understanding of other people's questions and ignorance, but with the grace of fortitude, I am able to speak up for my sons when they cannot, be it at a clinic appointment, individualized education plan meeting, or on the playground. I am often reminded of the Gospel story where parents are trying to bring their children to Jesus, and the disciples (otherwise good and holy men) are trying to keep the swarm of children away:

> And they were bringing children to him, that he might touch them; and the disciples rebuked them. But when Jesus saw it he was indignant, and said to them, "Let the children come to me, do not hinder them; for to such belongs the kingdom of God. Truly, I say to you, whoever does not receive the kingdom of God like a child shall not enter it." And he took them in his arms and blessed them, laying his hands upon them. (Mark 10:13–16)

I am blessed with a supportive parish that includes my sons whenever possible. If you are told your child cannot receive religious education, attend Mass, or enter into a building because of her disability, pray for fortitude and then demand justice, even if it makes others uncomfortable or upset. Good and holy people with the best of intentions can be wrong. Jesus became indignant when the children were kept from him — you have the right to speak up! Use your voice to rally others to your cause, and edu-

cate well-meaning but misguided people who are trying to prevent your child from receiving what God wants for him or her.

Trying to rely on perseverance and fortitude doesn't mean
there aren't times when I throw up my hands and think I don't
know how I can do it anymore. Practicing the virtues, however
imperfectly, means that when I fall down I can rally and get back
up again. Special-needs parenting can sometimes feel like you'll
be stuck doing the hard work of caring for your child forever,
and there's the fear that when you're gone, no one will be able
to take over your caregiving duties. The lifetime burden of your
child's care can feel overwhelming. But Jesus told us to "not be
anxious about tomorrow, for tomorrow will be anxious for itself.
Let the day's own trouble be sufficient for the day" (Mt 6:34).

Pray for the strength you need for that day, or that hour, or
the next ten minutes if need be. We are all insufficient instruments, but we can do the tasks God has laid before us.

• • •

Eight years later, after Fulton had suffered through thirty-six
continual hours of vomiting, we decided to take him to the hospital for IV fluids. I wanted to keep him home; I so desperately
wanted to avoid another hospital stay. However, regardless of my
feelings, I knew the right thing was to take him to the Emergency
Department at the Children's Hospital. Now well-known since
our first visit for that respiratory infection, we were whisked
through to a room in the ER where Fulton asked for anti-nausea
meds and endured an IV placement and blood draw without a
second glance. I updated the doctors and nurses for each shift
until an in-patient room opened up that night. The scenario had
become so familiar that Fulton fell asleep in no time at all. I had
packed snacks, pajamas, a book, and my laptop to pass the time;
I was prepared to stay until he stabilized and could tolerate eat-

ing and G-tube feeds again. In addition to Fulton's care, I never hesitated to ask for help so I could go get more food for myself. I emailed or chatted online with my older children at home, and they sent me hilarious memes and videos to make me laugh. As I stood with the staff during morning rounds the next day, I realized how much of the medical jargon I now understood. Certainly, Fulton and I did not want to be in the hospital, especially since it was Easter break, but we made the best of it, knowing it was what we needed to do. I had become the advocate my son needed, and a resource to the doctors and nurses. My son could simply relax and recuperate. With confidence in the Lord, and his constant help, I knew we'd be home soon.

## What You Can Do: Staying Spiritually Strong and Resilient

You've found the joy in each day, and have started practicing giving thanks in all things, but then a crisis erupts or there is a change in your child's condition. In times like these, we may resort back to behaviors that we relied on during the grieving process (anger, denial, bargaining, depression) as I did immediately following Teddy's diagnosis. But the other option is to practice the virtues of fortitude and perseverance. Either way, you must tackle this situation, but by cooperating with God's grace and choosing to accept whatever challenges arise, you will find an inner strength and determination to guide you through. Along with this strength, God will comfort you in your struggles, whereas resorting to anger, worry, sadness, or complaining often leaves us worse for wear and weary from the anguish. By allowing ourselves to be strengthened, we find our capacity for the work at hand increased and we are better prepared for the next challenge, and it will scare us less. We can learn to love the everyday tasks that some would call drudgery, and offer up our struggles while giving thanks that we are allowed this opportunity to care for our child and family in this way.

Fortitude and perseverance require a daily choice to trust and serve God with joy and thanksgiving. These are immensely hard choices on some days, but they get easier with practice and prayer. These choices may look like:

- Refusing to argue with a doctor, parish member, extended family, or your spouse, and instead waiting for, or scheduling, a calm moment to discuss your concerns.
- Making the decision to say a Hail Mary or other prayer every time you catch yourself complaining.
- When you feel frustration rising, remembering to tell your child you love him, naming something specific that you love, and sharing a hug.

Each day you choose to persevere with virtue, you are that much stronger for the next day.

---

## KEY TAKEAWAYS

- Pray for the virtues of fortitude and perseverance when circumstances arise that make you feel angry, scared, worried, or depressed.
- Choose to love the work in front of you, knowing that the more you decide to do so, the easier it becomes.
- Practicing fortitude and perseverance will give you the strength to speak up and advocate on behalf of your child.
- God wants you to find comfort in him. This is possible when you cooperate with his plan, rather than struggle against it.

## Aspirations: Short Daily Prayers to God

When you are stretched to your limits by the tasks at hand, and struggling to keep going, try saying these short prayers throughout the day whenever worry, doubt, or fear creeps into your mind. In the words of St. Francis de Sales:

> Aspire then frequently to God ... by short but ardent darlings of your heart; admire His beauty, invoke His aid, cast yourself in spirit at the foot of the cross, adore His goodness, address him frequently on your salvation, give your soul to Him a thousand times a day, fix your interior eye upon his sweetness, stretch out your hand as a little child to its father that he may conduct you ... make a thousand sorts of different motions of your heart to enkindle the love of God and excite within yourself a passionate and tender affection for your divine spouse.*

- Jesus, I trust in you.
- Lord Jesus Christ, have mercy on me.
- O God, put thy gladness into my heart.
- Help me, O Lord my God.
- Jesus, Mary, and Joseph!
- Mary our hope, have pity on me.
- O Mary, conceived without sin, pray for us who have recourse to thee.

---

*St. Francis de Sales, *Introduction to the Devout Life*, (Longmans, Green, and Co., 1891) New Edition.

# 5

# Help! I Need Somebody!

## *The Grace of Humility*

After Fulton's diagnosis, the phrases I heard most commonly from people familiar with SMA were, "My [friend] had a child with SMA. That child died."

I actually dreaded talking to people who were familiar with the disease because ultimately the conversation would lead to death. Although I learned in time that neither Fulton nor Teddy had the most severe form of SMA and were not likely to die in the next few years, the reality of SMA kept me from talking to other SMA parents for a long time. Even when I learned of older kids, teens, and adults with SMA, they all required ventilators and feeding tubes, and some didn't even have the strength to smile. I didn't want to imagine my happy boys with their long eyelashes and crazy hair unable to do anything for themselves.

Besides, I reasoned, I had a wonderful support network of friends and family. I didn't need to make a whole new set of friends just because I had children with special needs.

Even when my current support system didn't understand, or I needed to be strong for one of them because the thought of *my* child's diagnosis was too much for *them*, I tried to shoulder the entire weight of this burden alone.

My friends and acquaintances always wanted to help. When pressed for how someone could help us, I often just asked for prayers. I know many were disappointed with this answer, but for many months as I struggled with the stages of grief, I could not pray for myself, and their prayers sustained us. But so often people wanted to shove checks or cash in our hands, or organize fundraisers. Tony and I were quickly bombarded with generous offers, and we had to figure out how and when to accept. We felt like other families probably needed this money more than we did, and we worried that if we started accepting money, people would judge us for how we spent it.

People desperately want to help families who are going through a rough patch. As we found out, it's hard to ask for and accept help. It's humbling to admit you can't do it all; that the burden you carry is too great for one person or family. But just as it's a blessing to help others in charity while expecting nothing in return, it is also a blessing to let others help you with your cross, like Simon of Cyrene assisted Our Lord on the way to Calvary.

For all my insecurities about accepting help, financial and otherwise, I have never felt that doing so makes me, my husband, or our family weak in any way. Furthermore, I have never felt entitled — that people *ought* to help us because of our situation. No one should feel compelled to help our family because our children are disabled. Certainly, Christians are called to practice charity, but no one should feel obligated to make us the recipient of his or her generosity. Likewise, unless you've been on the receiving end of charity as we have, it can be hard to decide how to give; who most needs your help? But once the tables were turned, I learned that we all need help, just in different ways and at different times.

Sure, I've heard of corruption in large charitable organizations, but in local communities and in personal relationships I hope most people can find a nonjudgmental and unquestioning cycle of giving and receiving. If Christ could give us the ultimate gift of salvation through his crucifixion, knowing we aren't worthy (and that we would continue to insult him!), can't we learn to give to a family in need without first wondering whether or not the money is going toward an approved use?

As a family on the receiving end, it's easy to feel in perpetual debt to people. Although we know Christ died for us on the cross and wiped away all our sins with his sacrifice, he didn't do it so he could hold it over our heads for the rest of our lives. It was done out of love and as a gift. We should live our lives to be worthy of such a gift, and likewise I often feel I need to live a life as a special-needs parent who is worthy of all the blessings our family receives from so many through prayers and donations. In that way, humbly accepting gifts is making me holier. Likewise, we have to overcome our prideful human nature, which resists giving others the opportunity to share our burdens. When they share our burdens, they are given a chance to grow in holiness as well.

We learned that accepting help — financial, spiritual, and otherwise — was part and parcel of this special-needs life, and we learned to look for specific ways that people could help us in truly useful ways. I started to take note of what we really needed, what insurance would cover, and whether or not we could pay for the rest.

Early on, we knew Fulton would need a power wheelchair.

Our home was not accessible, and neither was our van. When friends asked about hosting a walkathon for our family, we knew we needed to accept in order to afford the modifications necessary to accommodate Fulton's new chair. So, around the one-year anniversary of his diagnosis, instead of ruminating on another year of missed milestones and what-ifs, we walked with friends and family and raised not only enough money to help pay for copays on medical equipment, but also enough to build a large deck and ramp that would allow Fulton to drive his chair from the van's new wheelchair lift into our home. Even with all that plus the job of widening our doorways, we still had funds in reserve for a few years. The first walkathon was so successful, we didn't need to hold another.

I took the walkathon as further proof that the support community around us was providing for us, and therefore I continued to resist going out to meet other special-needs parents. I made one attempt to attend a Muscular Dystrophy Association event where one of Fulton's doctors would be speaking. I awkwardly sat at a table with several other special-needs families who shared a bit about their children. I didn't bond with them, and while in line for the buffet I tried to make small talk with a woman and her older son who was driving a power chair. All I could notice was the chair and think about Fulton's own chair on order, and of course all I could blurt out were my thoughts about his wheelchair. I saw them exchange a look and I knew I'd committed a faux pas. Clearly, bonding with other parents of children with special needs was not going to be my thing. I could hardly keep up with the friends I did have; how could I make time for what I assumed would be a very sad and depressing group of new people?

And then one afternoon, three years after Teddy was born, while my children piled stacks of picture books on a small table in the children's section of our library, I sat knees to my chest in an undersized chair reading a book by a fellow blogger with tears pouring out of my eyes, and trying to not break into a full-on ugly cry.

As I read the book *Bloom* by Kelle Hampton, I relived much of my own pain and suffering as I absorbed her words about her daughter's birth and subsequent Down syndrome diagnosis. Obviously, our lives were not identical; but as I read reviews of her book on Goodreads and saw how poorly some people rated her book because of the feelings she shared — feelings I understood all too well — I finally realized the power of connecting with other special-needs parents. In my pride, I thought I understood what all special-needs parents, and friendships with them, would look like. *Bloom* handed me a new dose of humility, and I quickly warmed up to the idea of talking with and even learning from other special-needs parents. Overnight I went from avoiding SMA parents to seeking them out in groups on Facebook, and asking to be connected to moms who might have two sons with SMA, or be homeschooling.

Lo and behold, these parents weren't a sad, depressing group of people. Instead, these people understood the challenges I was facing on a daily basis and didn't judge me harshly when I complained, or put me up on a pedestal for all the times I was just loving my child.

Reading *Bloom* helped me understand I wasn't the only one with these struggles or thinking these thoughts. I was not alone and facing a completely new and unheard-of disease or struggle. The new normal our family had adopted wasn't strange to these people, and didn't evoke sympathy or looks of pity.

I took my humorous quasi-homeschooling blog and added a page about SMA, something I'd mentioned only briefly up to that point. I started to share some of the struggles and unique blessings that came with being a parent to children with special needs.

Again, I was not alone. Emails soon poured in from other special-needs parents looking to connect with other Catholic parents. Parents without special-needs children commented to let me know how much my writing opened their eyes to the challenges disabled people and their families faced on a daily basis. Not only did I learn that I needed to connect with other special-needs parents for my own benefit, but I needed to share our story to help other people. I'd felt for so long that my family would always need to be on the receiving end of charity, and that I had nothing of value to add to the world as a stay-at-home mom and caregiver. But now I realized that God had given me a unique platform, and a unique voice, to share with other struggling special-needs parents and those who wanted to learn more.

• • •

In 2014 I turned 35, and I finally felt that I needed to give back. Originally I thought about a huge black tie gala, but that was more work and expense than I could manage. So, although I hate running, I decided to run seven 5Ks for a total of what would become 35K for SMA. Tony's job was secure, our needs had been met, and it felt like time to pay it forward.

After years of needing so many prayers and donations of time and money, I was happy to find a way to help other families like ours who didn't have the same support network. I didn't want to start a charity, organize my own 5K, or reinvent the wheel, so simply choosing seven runs and raising money over the course of a year allowed me to donate more than $2,200 to four organizations that help SMA families purchase medical equipment. For one of the seven, I created a virtual 5K, and invited my readers to join me in raising money and awareness. I created a printable that proudly declared "I [fill in the blank] 5K for SMA!" People could run, walk, skip, or whatever they preferred, and then share a sweaty selfie with the printable on social media. Some ran around their neighborhoods, some on their treadmills, but as the pictures appeared on social media I felt such gratitude for the friends, family, and readers who, despite not knowing anyone with SMA except my family, would undertake the challenge and donate their time and money to my efforts. I was bringing together my non-special-needs parent friends to help those in my special-needs community.

You may feel you don't have anything to offer other families, or maybe that what you can offer isn't good enough or helpful enough. But a humble person recognizes that whatever talents they've received from God are enough, and that we are called to share and multiply those talents, not hide them in the ground. Pride is the opposite; it's doing what you want or what you think people need purely for attention or gratification. I wasn't forcing myself to run because I wanted a medal. I did it because I had a platform where such a crazy gimmick meant I could raise tangible support and awareness for families like mine. When you reach a place where you, as a special-needs parent, have something to offer other special-needs parents, don't let a misguided sense of humility stop you. Your experiences, or time, or whatever, can help so many other people. You don't need to write a book, start a blog, or run a race. God only wants you to use the talents he's given you, not anyone else. And using your talents to help others in whatever capacity is ultimately going to help you too.

It's not to say you won't still need help down the road, but helping other people will also aid you in your own journey. It's not prideful to take what you've learned and apply it to helping others; it's the boost that comes from finding another silver lining in the circumstances of your life. When you reach the point of acceptance and joy, there are still so many people who aren't there yet, and don't see all the blessings in their unique life. You get to provide emotional, physical, spiritual, and financial help to them.

I realized I had come full circle. Although there are still many times I feel completely overwhelmed by our situation and unequivocally unqualified to offer any useful advice or assistance, it was clear that helping others on their special-needs journey was the missing piece to my own healing. All of us, whether or not we're special-needs parents, can get wrapped up in the needs of our own family and become blind to the needs of those around us. I'd lived for years in a bubble, with my focus solely on my own children and my own struggles. During these hard times, Tony and I learned to humbly accept the help of others. As our days became more filled with joy and hope, we could reach outside our comfort zones and find ways to humbly share our advice, experience, and support with other special-needs parents who were still struggling, which ultimately aided in our own healing process as well.

• • •

In 2016 I was asked to speak at Edel, a Catholic women's conference held in Charleston, South Carolina. During the weekend, one of the conference organizers, Jen, interviewed me on her radio show, which was being broadcast live from the event. I was nervous, uncertain of what she'd ask and what I should say, and sweating buckets. My face was bright red as it tends to get when I'm embarrassed, nervous, or had too much red wine. Although the segment was only a few minutes, it felt like an eternity, and afterward I couldn't remember much of anything. I know I talked about being a special-needs parent and the difficult times immediately following the diagnosis of my sons (even though my talk at the conference had nothing to do with those things). Jen reassured me it went great. I took her at her word, then immediately resumed worrying about the talk I was giving later in the afternoon. I barely gave the radio interview a second thought until I arrived home and received an email from a radio listener.

Traci was a Catholic mom with two boys who had SMA. She lived in Charleston, but couldn't attend the conference because her husband was deployed, and when you've got two special-needs kids and are parenting solo, it's hard to spend the weekend at a conference.

I ran to find my husband with my laptop in my arms, the browser window opened to her email.

"Tony! Tony! There's another mom who has two boys with SMA! They're close in age to Fulton and Teddy! And she's Catholic!"

"Oh, that's great." He offered a smile, but clearly didn't understand the monumental significance of his extrovert wife finding the holy grail of special-need parent friends.

We didn't meet in person until two years later, but we maintained a close online relationship sharing stories and advice. Whenever I felt especially alone or isolated, I knew I could reach out to Traci and talk. She was someone who could sympathize in a unique way.

I didn't abandon my non-special-needs friends, but now I could share certain parts of my life with people who understood it, rather than talk to people who, while wanting to help, often didn't know what to say. I could now enjoy these friendships more because I wasn't carrying pent-up feelings of frustration that our struggles were different and no one could help me with them.

What I finally learned from my experience was that making friends in the special-needs community gave me an arena in which I could vent without judgment and get practical advice. ("Who has a letter of medical necessity for a bath chair they can share??") I could still enjoy my other friends and chat about the normal challenges of parenting, how to raise our children in the Faith, and our favorite cocktail recipes. If we needed financial, spiritual, or other support (child care, transportation, meals, etc.), I turned to my longtime friends and family who always were eager to help in any way they were capable of (versus trying to calm me down over a scary test result they didn't necessarily understand). I thought it would be harder to have a larger network of support, but I learned that each helped me in its own way, and conversely, my role in each was different. I still have friends and family who either pity me or put me on a pedestal. My special-needs community does neither. They understand my need to be viewed as a regular mom.

I went from avoiding special-needs parents, to reaching out to those I saw struggling, to recommending that newly diagnosed families seek out support (when they were ready). I went from struggling to process every request for financial aid to clearly articulating what we needed most, and when and why other items or donations were not a good fit for us; and I didn't feel guilty expressing those differences. Humility had taught me I couldn't do it all, and that was OK. I could step outside my comfort zone and get help, even from the most unlikely of places.

In our case, that meant the public school system. Throughout everything that had happened in the eight years since Fulton's diagnosis in 2009, I continued to homeschool. I went from a house of emerging readers and crayon masterpieces, to Latin exams and Shakespeare.

Every year presented its own unique challenges, but as Fulton continued to struggle with reading, I realized that his academic and physical needs were now eating up the bulk of my day, and our entire homeschool was struggling as a result. Tony and I decided to approach our local school district in early 2017 about enrolling Fulton and Teddy so they could hopefully diagnose why Fulton had such a hard time learning, and help Teddy, whose education had completely slipped through the cracks, catch up.

I wasn't eager to turn over control of my children's education to the school district, but I knew I needed help. I didn't feel guilty or like I was a failure because I couldn't do it all alone. The unexpected surprise was that the school district required Fulton to have a nurse, and shortly after he got nursing for school hours, he was approved for after-school hours and on the days he was off school too. Not only was my son cared for and educated by a whole team of teachers, aides, and nurses at school, but now I had another set of hands at home to help me out.

Trusting other people with the care of my children took time. Learning to let go of control has been an ongoing process; even as I think I've put all my trust in God, I realize I'm still clinging tightly to the reins and asking him to take a back seat to my plans. Sometimes my pride holds me back from the people I need, but thankfully I've learned with growing humility to see these people as the gifts from God that they actually are.

## What You Can Do: Embracing Help with Humility

You are not being asked to parent your special-needs child in a vacuum. God happily extends help to those who ask in the form of spiritual graces and other people. If you want to feel completely overwhelmed and miserable, then all you need to do is ignore everyone and anything that might help you, and hold on to the false belief that you can do it on your own, or worse, that God expects you to do it on your own. It's simply not true. It's more than likely there are people in your family, parish, community, workplace, and school who want to help you but don't know how. There are other parents who have children just like yours who are happy to talk and share their knowledge, or simply provide a listening ear.

Make a list of what you need help with; patience, affording

medical equipment, information on new treatment methods — any and everything that you haven't been able to manage on your own. Now look at all the people you know: Who can pray for you to grow in patience? Who can donate money or organize a fund-raiser? Who has the latest news on your child's diagnosis? Maybe you can name someone for each need, or maybe you need to cast your net outside your comfort zone and start meeting new people who can, and want, to help you as a special-needs parent. The resistance you feel toward reaching out for help is pride, and it can only be overcome through humility.

"Come to me, all who labor and are heavy laden, and I will give you rest. Take my yoke upon you, and learn from me; for I am gentle and lowly in heart, and you will find rest for your souls. For my yoke is easy, and my burden is light" (Mt 11:28–30). Our Lord wants us to do the work laid before us, as he did his work on earth — with a humble heart. When we carry our yoke with humility, with the help of others, we will find it lighter. Keep this list of needs handy so when someone offers help you know what to ask for. If you are not connected with other parents, use social media or a social worker at your local children's hospital to help connect you. Online groups especially provide an easy way to potentially find new friends around your caregiving and family life. Send emails, text or message people with children like yours. I'm never annoyed when I get an email from a new special-needs parent, and now I tend to go out and hunt them down at support group meetings and online groups to extend a warm welcome and a hug, whether virtual or in person.

You might find you have the voice other people need to hear, just as you need to hear theirs. Maybe the needs of your child are so great, helping others still seems impossible. But know that asking for help, allowing others to help you, and receiving help humbly is a powerful example in and of itself.

## KEY TAKEAWAYS

- Asking for and receiving help requires humility.
- Humbly accepting assistance is what makes our cross lighter.
- You are not weak because you need help.
- Helping your family gives others the opportunity to practice charity.
- All the people in your life can help you in different ways. Match your needs with the gifts of that person.
- Sharing your experiences and talents through writing, outreach, advocacy, and fundraising can potentially help other special-needs parents. Don't hesitate to share your story and connect with others.

### Prayer for the Embrace of Humility

Many of us can find it hard to humbly accept help from others; we want to do it all ourselves. However, God wants us to ask for and receive help to carry our crosses, just as his Son did on the way to Calvary. Use this prayer to help open yourself to assistance from others.

> Lord, I know that humility is good and is therefore good for me. I know that I must choose this virtue and so I do choose it. Please help my mind, heart, will, emotions and my entire being to be open to the beauty of this glorious gift. Help me to become convinced, with every fiber of my being, that humility is the foundation for a life of holiness and happiness. Soften my heart, purify my desires, and bring light to my mind, dear Lord. Give me the grace I need to choose to embrace the glorious gift of humility. Jesus, I trust in You.*

---

*https://mycatholic.life/books/the-path-to-holiness/ch-2-the-virtue-of-humility/.

# 6

# Loving Even When

## *The Grace of Charity*

I had found an outlet for myself, and the means to help others through my blog, but Tony and I now faced the challenge of taking care of our marriage amid the great needs of our children. We were no longer just husband and wife, or Mama and Papa, but caregivers to two medically fragile children, twenty-four hours a day, seven days a week. We had joked to each other as newlyweds that we would have all our children while we were young and then be empty nesters while we were still young enough to enjoy it. We envisioned living in an RV and driving around the country or retiring to a rustic cabin in the woods. We had to rethink our plans to potentially include two of our children, who required help to do everything, living with us their entire lives.

It was a warm Saturday morning in the early fall of 2016. As

Tony sat down in the chair across from me, I took a sip from my coffee and looked out across the front yard far into the neighboring farm field. The kitchen door was wide open, and through the screen our dog sat, whimpered, and wondered why she couldn't join us. There was no noise coming from the boys' bedroom, and Tony and I settled into our early morning routine of watching the sun from our small front porch.

"What's on your agenda for today?" I asked him.

"I need to mow and run to Lowe's for some supplies to finish the entry," he replied.

"Don't forget I need to run to the store and take the girls shopping," I said.

He sighed. "Well, I guess I won't get much done while you're gone."

"I'll hurry," I tried to assure him. "Maybe your dad could come over to mow."

"I'll do as much as I can before you leave," he answered.

Although speeding commuters on our road would sometimes drown out our conversation, or a neighbor walking a dog would send ours into a barking frenzy, these quiet mornings, for however many minutes we could manage before the boys woke up, were our alone time together.

Once someone was awake, the pace would be nonstop until Fulton and Teddy were in bed, or I passed out on the couch during family prayers, the older kids kissing me goodnight as they tucked themselves into bed. Being caregivers for Fulton and Teddy was sort of like having two children who never outgrew the newborn stage, except to loudly express their needs with a growing vocabulary or wheelchair nudge to the shins. Most parents care for their children for only a short time before those kids start doing more and more for themselves, eventually becoming young adults who leave the nest. Caregivers of mentally or physically disabled kids never get to step back and let their kids take over, because their children can't. For many, the constant level of attention and endless demands never go away.

For many years, date nights were near impossible. We were slow to trust family members with Fulton's nighttime routine as it evolved from BiPAP use and NG-tube feeds to occasional breathing treatments, night splints and G-tube feeds. Making alone time became something we did in brief two-hour spurts in the early afternoon or early evening, making sure to arrive home in time to put Fulton to bed. Occasionally, we would allow others to lay Fulton in bed, but we would hook up all his feeds and equipment when we got home. Of course, this only worked when he was healthy. Kid-free events required special planning because not just any old babysitter would do, and we couldn't leave the kids at just any house since most aren't wheelchair friendly. If we couldn't make it work, which was common, we just didn't go.

Raising and educating our children, plus meeting all of Fulton and Teddy's daily needs consumed my day. Tony worked a full-time job, commuted, and shared the work of child care and housework when he was home. Together in the evenings, our family was happy, if not loud, and so while date nights were rare, we were usually too busy and tired to wonder if everything was OK with our marriage. Even if we were struggling, what could we do about it? And when?

By making time for each other, even in the small windows that popped up — in the morning, or after everyone was in bed, on a walk around the neighborhood, or quick lunch date — we were able to keep enough of a pulse on our relationship to know if trouble was brewing. In the instances when we pushed concerns aside or didn't carve out those windows, we had some of the only arguments I can remember. It might have seemed at the time that those quiet mornings weren't all that special or important because they couldn't rival a long weekend away, but regular moments alone in earnest listening added up to hours, maybe days, of marriage fortification. We had to be intentional with our time together, not feel bad when we made time for one another, and make sure we continued to model a good Catholic marriage for our children. We were not only just caregivers for our sons, even though some days it might have felt like I had accomplished nothing else except keeping Fulton and Teddy alive and fed.

But lingering in the background was the struggle to adhere to the Church's teaching in regards to contraception and pregnancy. Tony and I now knew any future pregnancy would have a one in four chance of us having another child with SMA. As a happily married and affectionate couple, we struggled with the long periods of abstinence Natural Family Planning requires. And even once I had a better sense of my cycle (post-pregnancy and nursing with Teddy), the fear of another high-risk pregnancy and SMA child meant we still abstained for long periods of time, feeling already pushed to our limits by everything on our plate.

There was no question of whether we agreed with the Church — we did — but knowing the Church was right didn't make it any easier to do the right thing. I had to avoid conversations online and in person with Catholics who felt that, regardless of circumstances, you always had to be open to life and not sabotage your marriage with long periods of abstinence. Or that somehow I could use X method of NFP and then have all the sex we wanted with no pregnancies because the method was foolproof! And if I did get pregnant, clearly I did something wrong and I should be happy to be pregnant. The lack of intimacy, lack of alone time, and constant demands of our family could feel overwhelming at times to both of us.

We knew that we vowed through sickness and health, but I always took that to mean that one day, way in the future when we were really old, one of us would probably have to care for the other. I didn't expect sickness to enter our family via our children. I certainly didn't expect it to intrude into our bedroom.

We had to find new ways to show our love and make time for one another amid all the challenges in our life. We couldn't celebrate an anniversary by taking a spontaneous overnight to a bed and breakfast. We couldn't throw caution to the wind any time the mood struck unless we felt we could manage me being pregnant and on bedrest for months, and the care of another child with special needs on top of the two we had. Even if we trusted in God, we needed to exercise prudence beyond most couples we knew. Carelessly having sex and figuring everything would work out fine would have been thoughtlessness, not divine inspiration. Carefully considering each month whether or not it would be prudent to become pregnant required prayer and careful deliberation. Even when it comes to procreation, we are supposed to practice self-control. Doing the right thing was often hard, but it was one more hard thing we learned to do. In time, God helped us find peace with how we approached family planning, even if initially there was a lot of arguing with him.

Unfortunately, too many people think a man can't be expected to choose the good of his family over his own lust. There seemed to be an unspoken rule that my husband required a certain amount of sex or our marriage would suffer, or perhaps he'd turn to other mortal sins that would be my fault.

Because everyone had an opinion or advice, we shared this struggle with no one except our confessors as we struggled to balance our desire for holiness with our desire for each other. It was not until years later, when we finally reached a sense of peace and openness to God's plan, that I could open up and use our experience to help other special-needs parents wondering what God had in store for their marriages. In most of the emails I received through the years, family planning came up. For every

Catholic couple given a diagnosis, once they took a moment to stop worrying about their child, their next thought was future children. As I joined online groups and read the questions and comments, I saw the same questions popping up month after month — women wondering how open to life they needed to be when they were overwhelmed with a special-needs child, or children, or knew a future child may have the same condition. Secular doctors, friends, and family members couldn't understand the struggle, and casually replied to just use contraception or sterilize! Lots of faithful Catholics, just like Tony and me, were wrestling with applying the hard truths of the Faith to their everyday lives.

It took us five years to make peace with our fertility. I went from being terrified of being intimate with my husband and refusing almost all physical contact, to willingly abstaining whenever necessary while remaining open to any future surprises that may come along, confident we could tackle even another SMA child. I know that if you and your spouse can stick it out and do the hard work your faith demands, you too can find that same place of acceptance, relieved that you haven't done anything foolish or permanent. I encourage you to continue to find ways to love one another, and to not write off all future children right now in the midst of learning about a new diagnosis. Even if future children are not an option, God can strengthen you for that decision.

Marriage and raising a family is hard work, and now more than ever did I clearly understand that love toward my husband and children was a verb, an action, and not just a feeling I had toward them. I actively sought new ways to show my love to my husband, and I tried to incorporate a more active love for my kids into my time with them, whether it was during school, bath time, or breathing treatments.

True love is a sacrifice, modeled perfectly by Christ. When

we are able to view our trials as the result of love, and therefore inherently good, rather than senseless suffering, we've moved closer to what Christ suffered greatly, both physically and mentally, as he bore the sins of mankind on the cross. He did that for love of you and me, so I'm pretty sure I can handle sleepless nights and short walks alone instead of dinners out with my husband, though I'll admit patiently enduring trials is a constant struggle due to our sinful nature.

Suffering under the weight of love, when done right, gives us hope, makes us stronger, and opens us to God's grace. I think love is why I can continually bear up under the weight of SMA and not be crushed by it. Living a life focused on charity toward my husband and family gave me the strength I needed to overcome the challenges to my marriage, and helped me see the value in my daily caregiving, not the drudgery.

• • •

Tony and I hadn't been alone together for more than a few hours in almost ten years. The months and weeks leading up to this moment were fraught with a mix of anxious anticipation and nervous apprehension. Our older three children were enjoying time alone with my parents, and both Fulton and Teddy were under the care of the volunteers, nurses, and doctors of the MDA camp run by our local MDA office. Fulton was a veteran, with two years of camp under his belt already and a reputation for being Mr. Popular and the camp prank master. Teddy was young, and scared, and teared up as we pulled away. I knew that if the camp staff could successfully manage Fulton's care, they could tackle Teddy's — but would he let them? Should we have pushed Teddy to go to camp when he obviously wasn't excited? Fulton was glad to have his brother with him, and I knew he would help Teddy get acclimated. With five full days sans kids ahead of us, Tony and I planned to enjoy ourselves as much as possible and prayed all five kids would make it through the week without injury, illness, or homesickness.

The day after MDA camp drop-off, Tony and I walked up onto the Atlantic City boardwalk and felt the June sun and warm breeze on our faces. LED signs flashed advertisements, gulls screamed overhead, and the ocean roared in front of us.

"What do we do first?" I asked.

"I don't know!" Tony replied.

"I feel like we're getting away with something criminal!"

"I know, like any moment someone's going to come along and scold us for doing something we shouldn't."

We settled for sitting at an open-air casino bar, and sipped mojitos to kick off our first overnight trip alone.

Despite having to deal with numerous calls from the camp as Teddy struggled with homesickness, it was an amazing week. Tony and I shared the best parts of our day, and not just the tired and ragged edges with each other. We didn't need to rush through meals or walks to keep our date on schedule; we had the whole week. Our attention was never suddenly pulled away from one another or given in half-hearted bursts. I became convinced that while we had done a pretty good job of making time for each other up to that point, being offered complete respite was something we didn't even know we needed. MDA camp remains the one time every year we enjoy such a break.

When I made my wedding vow, I knew there might be tough times ahead, but I had the vague notion that love would magically fix everything. But love is not some outside magical force repairing people and relationships and strengthening them in times of trouble. That is the work of God, and it is only possible when we open ourselves to his love, and allow it to transform us to do the work laid before us in our families, parishes, and communities. When the mushy romantic feelings fade, and you're left with your spouse and his or her flaws, and you welcome several more flawed, tiny humans (able and possibly disabled) into your life, you can't rely on feelings to see you through. Those feelings of anger, helplessness, frustration, impatience, sadness, and hopelessness can overtake you if you don't choose to embrace your situation and love it, mess and all.

By making the effort to consciously love and make sacrifices for each other, even when we don't feel like it, we have created a loving home for not only each other, but all our kids. When we model love and care for Fulton and Teddy, all our kids see what true love encompasses. They see the hard times, but they see a resilient and loving marriage.

All marriages eventually move beyond the honeymoon phase and require hard work to continue. With a special-needs child, a marriage based on feelings and not mutual sacrifice can suffer tremendously, or not survive at all. Spouses have to embrace a sacrificial giving of themselves — charity in its purest form — not only to get their marriage healthy, but to safeguard it against future surprises.

## What You Can Do: Showing Charity Toward Your Spouse and Children

A marriage requires hard work from any couple, but couples blessed with a special-needs child could find themselves woefully unprepared for the challenges ahead. Despite limited time and the additional stress of parenting a child with a disability, special-needs parents need to carve out time for their marriage. Each spouse must not only work through their own emotions regarding their child's diagnosis, but also work with the other to create a loving and safe home for all their children. This may require outside counseling from a priest or trained therapist.

Couples need to acknowledge if their marriage is struggling and their current means of coping and communication are falling short. Investing in the health of your marriage is just as important as investing in the health of your child and yourself. All three require work and a concerted effort, or they don't happen. Too often in special-needs families, it's the marriage component that gets the short end of the stick.

Even couples with a healthy relationship need to make sure they set aside time to be alone and check in with one another, especially following a change in their child's condition or other related circumstances (a change of insurance with a new job, trouble getting the necessary accommodations at school, dealing with a particularly challenging doctor, etc.). Don't let the stress of special-needs parenting spill into your marriage. Build up your marriage so the love that thrives there can spill into all the other aspects of your life.

Love requires action and daily sacrifice; it's not something that happens on its own. How are you showing love to your spouse on a regular basis? When you feel stressed and overwhelmed, are you still able to show love? Does your spouse know how to support you and show love to you? If finding the time to have these conversations is hard, look into respite care so you can devote more time to your marriage. Ask at your child's school, the hospitals where he's treated, organizations that help children with his diagnosis, and local and state government programs for assistance in locating respite. Maybe there's another special-needs family who could take care of your child for an evening, and you extend the same to them on a different night.

Through the years, my husband and I have relied on numerous strategies to carve out time for ourselves: We would wake up early and drink coffee together; we'd stay up after the kids were in bed and share a dessert or drink; when grandparents were over, we'd take a walk around our yard or the block, or put on a movie and go to a bookstore for an hour. When one of our sons is in the hospital, we make sure to sit together and talk over the most recent developments while our child is resting or occupied with the TV. There were a few times friends and family came in and allowed us to step out of the room together to get a meal. Because we always prioritized time together, we could find creative ways to get at least five minutes alone, or at least undisturbed. Keep your eyes open for time you can spend together. Schedule it in advance when you can, and guard that time, remembering it's an investment in your marriage, not an indulgence. Seize those five-minute chunks whenever they arise and enjoy them without guilt. In some seasons of your life they will be almost impossible, which is why it's even more important to make time when your family isn't in survival mode.

The teachings of the Church in regard to family planning and contraception may be hard to follow. There's no way to sugarcoat that reality. Turn to a knowledgeable and orthodox priest or spiritual director to counsel you and your spouse if you're not sure how to proceed. You don't need to abstain for the rest of your married life, or be open to having as many babies as possible. There is a middle ground that can be determined only by the two of you, with prayer, spiritual guidance, and as little input from social media as possible.

---

## KEY TAKEAWAYS

- Make time to be alone, even for brief periods. Your unique situation will require unique solutions.
- Love requires action and Christ-like suffering, not just feelings.
- With God's help, you can choose to love even when you don't feel like it.
- Seek out opportunities for respite so you can devote more time to strengthening your marriage.
- When planning for future children, consult a knowl-

edgeable priest to help determine what God may be asking of you. Pray for prudence.

## Prayer to the Holy Family

Struggling couples need only look to the Holy Family for an example of how a marriage can thrive in the midst of hardship. Despite raising the Son of God, Mary and Joseph were not spared suffering, and instead were asked to endure great trials and sorrows. Ask for their intercession to strengthen your marriage.

O Jesus, only-begotten Son of the Eternal Father, well-beloved Son of the Blessed Virgin and foster Child of St. Joseph, we most fervently implore Thee, through Mary Thine ever-blessed Mother and St. Joseph Thy foster father, take our children under Thy special charge and enclose them in the love of Thy Sacred Heart. They are the children of Thy Father in Heaven, created after His own image; they are Thy possession, for Thou hast purchased them with Thy Precious Blood; they are temples of the Holy Ghost, who sanctified them in Baptism and implanted in their hearts the virtues of faith, hope and charity.

O most loving Jesus, rule and guide them, that they may live according to the holy Catholic Faith, that they may not waver in their confidence in Thee and that they may ever remain faithful to Thy love.

O Mary, Blessed Mother of Jesus, grant to our children a place in thy pure maternal heart! Spread over them thy protecting mantle when danger threatens their innocence; keep them firm when they are about to stray from the path of virtue; and should they have the misfortune of falling into mortal sin, oh, then raise them up again, reconcile them with thy Divine Son and restore them to Sanctifying Grace.

And thou, O holy foster father St. Joseph, do not abandon our children! Protect them from the assaults of the wicked enemy and deliver them from all dangers of soul and body.

O dear parents of the holy Child Jesus! Intercede for us parents also, that we may bring up our children in the love and fear of God and one day attain with them the Beatific Vision.

Amen.[*]

---

[*]https://www.catholic.org/prayers/prayer.php?p=1378.

# 7
# Learning from Each Other

## *The Grace of Understanding*

In 2018 I was asked to participate in a series of new special-needs parent support meetings hosted by the nursing agency that provided Fulton with care. These meetings had a few "veteran" special-needs parents, plus parents whose children had just been diagnosed. They were led by my friend, Shelby, a special-needs mom herself, who had told me all those years ago that I would smile again. After her own son had passed away, she dedicated her time to helping other parents of children with special needs through various roles. When she asked me to attend the meetings, despite the distance, I tried to attend occasionally.

At one meeting, the topic of siblings came up — as in, the typically developing siblings of special-needs kids. Several parents mentioned their concerns about how their typical kids

119

were doing, and our host, Shelby, mentioned how it was only in hindsight that she realized how much support her oldest daughter needed following her son's sudden diagnosis. It's easy to get wrapped up in the care of one child, and miss the struggles of our other kids. I was caught off guard. It had never occurred to me that my three older children might need help to process their feelings around Fulton and Teddy's diagnosis. It was their early love and acceptance that helped guide Tony and me forward on our own healing journey. What if somehow I'd missed out on their cries for help?

I sped home from the meeting and burst into the schoolroom, where my older two were up late working on homework, and blurted out, "Do either of you want counseling related to being the siblings of Fulton and Teddy? Do you feel like you have emotional needs that have not been met through the years because I spent so much time taking care of Fulton and Teddy?"

They both looked at me, totally caught off guard, wondering what to say. Finally Byron answered.

"No, I'm good."

Addie started to answer sarcastically about what she would tell her therapist one day, but upon realizing I was serious, she said, "No. Why would I need counseling related to Fulton and Teddy?"

After they insisted a few more times that they were fine, I exhaled and went to bed relieved.

Fulton's hospitalizations drove home to them that SMA was more than racing wheelchairs. As they approached their teenage years, I had sometimes wondered how being the siblings of two disabled brothers would shape them. They could now understand the severity of their brothers' conditions and see the real challenges that lay in store for Fulton and Teddy and Tony and me.

Some folks assumed Addie, Byron, and Edie would naturally grow into more loving and caring adults having grown up with disabled siblings, and would tell me this every time one of the older kids did something, anything, for one of their younger brothers while we were out in public. I wanted to believe this, especially on the days I felt I couldn't give enough of myself to everyone.

Occasionally I worried they would grow bitter with years of perceived neglect from me. Would they resent me and their brothers in time, or struggle in their own faith as they watched Fulton, and later Teddy, struggle with tasks they took for granted? I kept watching for signs of angst, but thus far they have not emerged. Perhaps because all they know is having a family with two wheelchairs, they cannot imagine otherwise. They gladly help with the boys; however, they are not on call twenty-four hours a day the way Tony and I are. I can count on them when I need them, but I give them each space from one another and time and resources to pursue their own interests.

They are all loving and compassionate and can often provide the voice of reason when I am too frustrated or angry about a situation. They continue to treat their brothers like typical kid brothers; there is a lot of potty humor correction, practical joke planning, and screaming when a wheelchair drives unannounced into the girls' room.

This impromptu interrogation following the support group meeting seemed to confirm what I already hoped: that our typical kids had come to see the realities of SMA, but it didn't shake their love and acceptance of Fulton and Teddy.

I believe it helped that, from a young age, our kids quickly realized that our family was different: We had more kids, we homeschooled, we were really Catholic (like "process around the yard blessing it with holy water" Catholic), we didn't have a TV, and Tony and I didn't care if people thought any of that was weird. Two boys in wheelchairs made us that much weirder, but we just didn't have time to worry what people thought. If Tony and I were confident in what we were doing, or at least acted that way, why should our older kids believe that anything was wrong? They taught us love and acceptance in those first couple of years, and we kept at it following their example, creating a self-fulfilling prophecy.

For years they didn't understand why everyone stared at Fulton and Teddy when we went out; now they do, but they don't feel ashamed. As they watch families around us end in divorce, or learn about the background of a child being fostered by a parish family, they feel blessed by our unusual family the same way Tony and I do.

One evening on the way to fencing class, I asked Addie if she ever felt deprived because she had more siblings than the average child (and by average I mean everyone else at the fencing school). Did she ever feel like she was forced to give up stuff because she had more siblings and two with special needs? She looked at me with the expression of a typical teen who feels their time has been wasted with an obvious question for which I should already know an answer.

"No. I mean, maybe if I was an only child I'd have my own room and an iPhone."

"I think you know we'd never get you an iPhone even if you were an only child."

"That's probably true."

End of discussion. She went back to reading.

These conversations with my teens helped me realize how selfish I either still am, think my kids are, or realize I was back when I was their age. Their lives are so very different from mine, it's unfair for me to assume they would react as I assume I would have. But I also need to make sure I don't assume that they're always fine.

Tony and I didn't always understand the whys of our life,

but after working through the stages of grief we learned that joy, peace — all of it — was possible by relying on faith without understanding the whys. Our young children didn't ask why, they just accepted two more siblings with open arms, and we learned to do the same. Moving past the whys allowed us to focus on the more important questions (How will we manage this? What does this require? Who can we ask to help?), and gain wisdom and perspective as special-needs parents. And as we grew in wisdom, we gained understanding of God's larger plan, even when the details eluded us. We understand Fulton and Teddy are happy and perfect as they are, and that God can bring good from their lives and their disabilities, even though initially we didn't believe this.

As my older, typically developing children grew up, they accepted Fulton and Teddy without hesitation, and as they matured, understood that the love between family isn't dependent on abilities and can adapt as circumstances require. We've all come to understand that happiness isn't confined to a very specific type of life. I don't know if Tony and I were conscientiously trying to pass on this perspective, or more that it arose organically from how we began to approach special-needs parenting once we left the stages of grief behind.

## What You Can Do: Understanding
Teenagers aren't known for being the most open with their feelings. If you are able to hold full conversations with them, check in frequently, especially following any period of illness, surgery, or change in your special-needs child's condition. If you don't think they're willing to talk to you, get a trusted adult to follow up with them, or speak to their school counselor. Watch for changes in their academic performance, appetite, and relationships with friends, family, and their siblings.

Younger children may act out in different ways: Tantrums,

regressions, and problems with sleep can all signal a child struggling with the big emotions that having a special-needs sibling can create.

There are siblings who need counseling or support groups at a young age to help them deal with and process their feelings related to being the sibling of a severely mentally or physically disabled child. Our children grew up with disabled brothers; they were young and welcomed Fulton and Teddy at an early age with no hesitation. It helps that Fulton and Teddy can interact with them socially at age-appropriate levels. For children whose siblings cannot interact with them, may be hostile or violent, or who have become disabled through a traumatic accident, it is important for special-needs parents to make the effort to check in frequently with their typical children and make sure they are OK and able to process their big emotions. Your children may go through their own stages of grief. Be on the lookout for the same signs given in the first chapter.

Giving dedicated one-on-one time, even in short ten-to-fifteen-minute bursts, can mean a lot to any child. Just as the time you give your special-needs child shouldn't always be directed toward their caregiving, all the time you give your typical children shouldn't be shared with the caregiving of your other child(ren). Consider reading a story alone to one child in bed, taking one child with you when running errands, having a different "kitchen helper" each night at dinner time, or turning the drive to sports practice into something special with an occasional drive-through run. I have one child who loves crafts, and so being creative together for an hour a week was our special time for a while. I also can usually convince someone to take a short walk with me. Another child loves staying up late, and sitting with her on the couch, even when I'm dead tired myself, is a great way to connect one on one. If you're stuck for ideas, just ask your children! Usually they have plenty of ideas for how they'd like to spend time with you.

There are more and more sibling support groups forming for kids whose siblings have special needs. Ask your kids if they'd like to join such a group, or consider forming a group if you know many typical siblings among your special-needs friends.

If your children assist with caregiving, check in with them to make sure they are comfortable with the level of help you are asking of them, and make sure you don't take their help for granted. Chances are they are happy to help, but everyone likes the occasional thank you. You also don't want to expose your kids to aspects of your disabled child's care that they're not ready for. My teens can now perform most of the tasks Fulton needs during the day, but that wasn't the case immediately. And when Fulton was recovering from surgery, we didn't require them to do more than they already were.

If they need a break, give them one. Allow them to say no to assisting you at times. They are kids and siblings first and foremost. If you find yourself needing their help all the time, and struggling without it, chances are you need to bring in outside help. Allow your typical children to just playfully interact with their disabled sibling just as they do with other typical siblings or children. If they want to do something else, or your disabled child isn't playing nice, then don't force your typical child to endure behavior you wouldn't. My teens are usually more than happy to play with Fulton and Teddy, but when the older ones have homework, I let them do their homework, not play games so I can take a break. If Fulton and Teddy start making demands, acting rude, or interrupting one of their older siblings, I don't expect my teens to tolerate that behavior just because Fulton and Teddy are disabled. Tony and I ask our teens if they mind watching the boys so we can go out; we don't assume they'll do it, and we pay them for babysitting. Make sure there are clear expectations between your typical kids and you and your spouse so everyone's preferences are respected.

---

**KEY TAKEAWAYS**
- Following a diagnosis for one of your children, watch for signs of distress in your other children.
- Make sure you continue to give your typically developing children one-on-one time.
- Make outside counseling or sibling support services available if needed.
- Allow your typical children to help care for their special-needs sibling as age and interest allow.
- Allow your typical kids and children with special needs to find their own normal play relationship with each other.
- Check in with your typical children as they age, and watch for signs of anxiety, stress, resentment, etc., that may require outside intervention. If they won't talk to you, find someone with whom they can talk.
- Don't force your typical children to be caregivers to their special-needs sibling.

**Prayer to the Holy Spirit**
Since one of the gifts of the Holy Spirit is understanding, it seems fitting to call upon the Third Person of the Trinity to assist us, and our typically developing children, in understanding our relationship with our special-needs children. Guided by this gift, and the others the Holy Spirit will bestow on us, we can hope the sibling bonds our children experience will bless them throughout their lives, and provide an opportunity for practicing virtues.

Holy Spirit, Divine Spirit of light and love, I consecrate to you my understanding, heart, and will, my whole being, for time and for eternity. May my understanding be always submissive to your heavenly inspirations and to the teaching of the Catholic Church, of which you are the infallible Guide. May my heart be ever inflamed with the love of God and of my neighbor. May my will be ever conformed to the Divine Will. May my whole life be faithful to the imitation of the life and virtues of our Lord and Savior Jesus Christ, to whom with the Father and you be honor and glory forever.

God, Holy Spirit, Infinite Love of the Father and the Son, through the pure hands of Mary, Your Immaculate Spouse, I place myself this day, and all the days of my life, upon your chosen altar, the Divine Heart of Jesus, as a sacrifice to you, consuming fire, being firmly resolved now more than ever to hear your voice and to do in all things your most holy and adorable will.*

---

*Fr. Lawrence G. Lovasik, SVD, *Favorite Novenas to the Holy Spirit: Arranged for Private Prayer* (Totowa, NJ: Catholic Book Publishing, 1997).

# 8
# Remember the "Present"

## *The Grace of Prudence*

The surgeon brought the x-ray up on the screen, showing a spine curved and bent like a macaroni noodle. "Now is the time to do something. We need to think about surgery."

Fulton's ears perked up.

"When are you thinking? This year? How soon?" I asked.

"This summer ideally."

I let out a long sigh.

"Wait, am I getting surgery today?" Fulton exclaimed with wide eyes.

"No, bud," the doctor reassured him, "but I'm going to talk to Mom and Dad about bringing you back soon to fix your back. The brace just isn't cutting it anymore."

• • •

We knew since Fulton was a toddler that he would eventually need back surgery. Because of all-over muscle weakness, his spine would curve, contorting his body, and ultimately compressing the lung on one side of his chest, making breathing harder and respiratory infections even more dangerous. Within the SMA medical community, there are several options to treat spinal curvature. We decided, on the advice of a neurologist at Johns Hopkins in Baltimore who we saw through the early years of the boys' diagnoses, to put Fulton (and later Teddy) in body braces that would support their upper body and hopefully prevent their spines from curving too much too soon. The goal was to put off the surgery until Fulton was ten or older, at which point we could just do a spinal fusion in one surgery. If the curve became too severe and he needed surgery sooner, they would have to put metal rods in his back along the spine, and then go in every few months to adjust the rods so he could grow a bit taller (meaning multiple surgeries and all the risks that come with that). But at age ten, we could safely fuse the spine and avoid additional surgeries.

From age two on, Fulton was fitted for body braces every six months or so. While we visited Hopkins, the doctors were happy with his progress. However, our local Children's Hospital of Philadelphia, where he was seen by other specialists, did not approve of the body brace method, and we faced constant opposition from them. They wanted to do surgery right away, and at every check-up a note was made in Fulton's file about their recommendations against the brace and in favor of surgery.

In 2014 our insurance changed and the boys could no longer be followed at Hopkins. Tony and I wrestled with what to do. To move Fulton's spine care to Children's Hospital would mean surgery sooner rather than later, and probably multiple surgeries. We needed to find a hospital that supported the use of body braces and would work with our insurance. Initially, we managed to get prescriptions for the braces written by the boys' primary doctor while we tried to find a surgeon. Unfortunately, with his current brace getting small and more uncomfortable, I worried that if we couldn't find something soon, his spine might radically change, and we'd be too late getting him a new doctor.

We also doubted our decisions. What if we were wrong? What if Hopkins was wrong? What if we were making a horrible decision to brace him and delay surgery?

We were making decisions for our child that would impact his quality of life for the rest of his life. No matter what we chose, there were risks, big scary risks, and Tony and I would have to take full responsibility for them for the rest of our lives.

Finally, after some research into types of back surgery, I came upon Shriners Hospital of Philadelphia, and we visited there in 2016. They supported bracing, relieved our fears by confirming that Fulton's spine did not need surgical correction at that time, and agreed with delaying surgery as long as we could to reduce the number of potential surgeries. At that point Fulton was eight, and we didn't have that much longer to go until we hit the ten-year benchmark. Even though we knew the day was quickly approaching, we were still surprised when we learned it had actually arrived.

• • •

There are still plenty of times when I feel the same as my sixteen-year-old self and wonder, how is it possible that I'm a responsible adult and have all these kids dependent on me? What made God think I was capable of this job?

With Fulton and Teddy, I am now forced into what I consider extreme adulting mode because I have to make such big scary decisions about their care. It's not the normal bumps, bruises, and broken bones you deal with in other children. And the things I need to force Fulton and Teddy to do for their own good go beyond the normal chides to "Eat your vegetables!" or "Did you wash your hands with soap?"

I know I made mistakes with my older children in regard to how I disciplined or homeschooled them, but they are happy teens who I expect will go on their merry way from under my wings and forge their own path, no worse for having lived with an anxious and uncertain mother for a few years. But with Fulton and Teddy, decisions about care, education, or pretty much anything loom large because everything seems riskier. When I considered putting Fulton in school, due to undiagnosed learning disabilities that had made homeschooling him almost impossible, I had to carefully weigh the risk of coming in contact with more germs and the increased likelihood of respiratory infections and hospitalizations. I could send my older children out into the yard to run mostly unsupervised and only worry if I heard blood-curdling screaming. But with Fulton and Teddy, a wheelchair could break down or become stuck, leaving them stranded or worse, a risky driving maneuver (Teddy!) could potentially flip it over or break it. If my older kids got in fights with each other or friends, I never intervened. But Fulton and Teddy can't stop an angry child from messing with their wheelchair controls, and can't raise their arms to defend themselves. Driving away in a wheelchair is a lot slower than most kids can run. I had to become a helicopter parent in some ways and questioned interactions I'd never given a second thought to before.

I wanted them to have the same independent, free-range-type childhood of their siblings, but in most ways that was impossible. I didn't want to worry about them more, but I did. I didn't want to treat them differently, but I did.

I thought I had parenthood all figured out by the time Fulton arrived, and then he and Teddy flipped everything I held as Gospel upside-down. I was starting over and figuring out a new set of rules as I went along.

Even family fun required diligence. Packing for vacations required a three-page checklist and evaluating every rest stop and attraction for accessibility. Sometimes we had to wonder if all the extra hassle and cost was worth it: Wouldn't it be easier to stay home? Spontaneous day trips decreased as the boys' weights increased. It was getting too hard to carry them onto the beach, or up a flight of stairs in their medical strollers, or find an accessible parking spot in a busy downtown area. One time I came home from a beach day trip and cried; it had been so hard, and exhausting, I feared the days of me taking all the kids to the beach solo were over. I didn't want to admit I couldn't do it all myself anymore. I didn't want to face that our lifestyle was changing. We could certainly find joy in the activities we chose to do as a family, but we had to admit that some activities were now more trouble than they were worth. Tony and I had to mentally prepare ourselves for extended trips that would inevitably exhaust us because of constantly trying to make do with inaccessible or less than adequate accommodations and attractions.

I realized I couldn't make the same assumptions about their futures. I never worried about outliving my children until I had two with special needs. When surgeries or hospitalizations arose, I automatically thought of worst-case scenarios: having to bury my child and carrying on with my life without them.

While they would talk about future careers (scientists, police officer, etc.), I wondered when and how they could ever live independently. Would they find a spouse who would love them and take on the work of being their caregiver? Would I be able to turn over the work of caregiving to a potential daughter-in-law? Would they have children of their own? Would they leave behind a young widow? What if they outlived me and didn't have a spouse? Who would care for them?

These were only some of the questions that would race through my mind if I sat and thought for any length of time about my sons' futures, so usually it was a subject I avoided thinking about at all costs. These worries served no purpose except to keep me up at night. But by avoiding these worries, I also didn't do anything practical to prepare for the future, which meant it remained a big scary unknown that I just hoped would figure itself out.

• • •

As we left the exam room at Shriners and headed home, the reality of surgery hit me square between the eyes. On one hand, Tony and I were happy; we'd made it to the point of Fulton only needing one surgery! When spinal surgery was brought up years ago, the age of ten had seemed a lifetime away, but suddenly here we were. Fulton would be turning ten in a few months, and while the surgery meant he would stop getting taller, he would no longer wear a brace, and he would be able to sit tall in his wheelchair without an external support device. Fulton was also getting Spinraza, a new medicine that was making him stronger and preventing the weakening of his muscles, via lumbar puncture every four months. With a strong spine and continued doses, Fulton would hopefully not face the same future of many of the young adults I saw with SMA who required much more breathing and nutritional support, and sat slumped and crooked in their chairs (which is still a great life to have versus no life at all, but one that I was glad Fulton could avoid).

On the other hand, it was surgery, major surgery that would put him under anesthesia and intubated for about eight hours. His recovery would be painful, and there were risks of infection, and of the hardware in his back breaking, and of scar tissue making future Spinraza doses difficult or impossible. He would not be able to go to school for at least six weeks. In order to accommodate new, safer ways of transferring Fulton we would need to rearrange the boys' bedroom, and Teddy would need to temporarily sleep somewhere else in our house. The what-ifs in my mind started in immediately, but this time I couldn't push them away. Fulton needed surgery now before the curvature in his spine got worse and left him permanently slouched and at greater risk of respiratory infections.

• • •

The future arrives one way or another. We can be prepared, or let it catch us unaware.

In every other aspect of life, I'm a researcher and a planner. I thoroughly investigate whatever needs doing, and then make a plan on how to accomplish it. But for some reason, up to the point of Fulton's surgery, I'd set aside that tendency and avoided dealing with the harsh realities of my sons' diagnoses. I did what we needed to do, followed doctors' orders, and obviously loved and cared for my boys, but I did not follow research studies, advocacy groups, or pay attention to events designed to specifically help me plan for my boys' futures. I didn't want to read or learn anything unpleasant in my quest to find joy in my day, so I didn't do more than what was necessary. I would fill out mountains of paperwork so they could go to summer camp (fun! joy! happy memories!), but would avoid taking steps to set up a special-needs trust after attending a free seminar on the topic (sadness! death!).

What I didn't realize then was that planning for the future and worrying about it are two completely different things. By educating ourselves and planning, we can often lay aside the worry. We can find peace in knowing we've done the best we can, and trust God with the unexpected. We can learn to not second-guess our decisions because they weren't made in haste or based on our emotional state, but were based on the information we had at the time.

In addition to the practical details that surround planning for surgery, or long-term care, are the spiritual details. If your special-needs child is still very young, think about how they will receive religious education and their sacraments, and what accommodations, if any, will be made for them. Is your parish accessible for them? As your child grows, will you still be able to attend the same church, or are there physical barriers that could be addressed now? Remember the Sacrament of Anointing of the Sick; schedule it before any procedure rather than arrive at the hospital without that extra grace.

Ultimately, I learned that with thorough, prayerful planning came more enjoyment and peace, even if things were still harder. I learned how to eliminate activities that drained me and frustrated the boys and didn't feel guilty about it. There are too many fun things we can do to feel sorry about what we can't. (If other people were upset that we couldn't attend an event or participate, that was their problem. It's ridiculous to expect a special-needs family to accommodate everyone else.) By planning for and learning to enjoy things like vacations and day trips, I saw that if planning made things easier and the trips less stressful, I could take that same rationale and apply it to big scary things like surgery too.

There's a lot more uncertainty with planning for the big things, so there's a lot more trusting in God that needs to happen. When things go wrong on vacation, it sucks, but it's not the end of the world. When things go wrong with a medical intervention, it could literally be a matter of life and death. Planning out to the best of my ability, with the help of doctors and trusted special-needs parents, often means the concerns no longer need to take up space in my head.

As the boys got older and asked more of their own questions ("Why can't I walk?" "Will I walk when I grow up?" "Why do I need a G-tube and BiPAP?"), I tried to be honest and share information about SMA, but not overwhelm them with grim statistics of the future. The last thing I wanted was for them to worry. If I felt anxious and concerned with the future, or expressed only sadness at what might happen, they certainly would too. I can't promise them that they'll walk — more than likely they never will — but I can point out all the things they can still do now and as adults. I can give them hope that the same medical technology that designed their chairs, helps them heal from respiratory infections, and would straighten Fulton's back, could one day figure out a way to help them do things they currently can't. There are adults with SMA who are married, have children, and live independently. When I start to worry, I remember all the disabled people living happy lives. I might not know now how Fulton and Teddy will achieve all their goals (which currently involve owning competing multibillion-dollar comic book companies), but with all my children there is uncertainty. Raising confident kids who can advocate for themselves and fight for their dreams wasn't something I could do if I allowed myself to incessantly dwell on the unknowns. For the sake of my family, I couldn't remain a worrier.

• • •

The day of surgery approached. I had a checklist of what to take to the hospital. Fulton had received Anointing of the Sick the previous Sunday. We'd sent out specific prayer requests to anyone and everyone we knew. Family and friends carried those requests even further. I read up on what to expect, I asked questions, I lined up help at home. When I started worrying about worst-case scenarios, I asked for more prayers. When they wheeled him back, I was as ready as I could have been, still concerned for my son and the painful recovery yet to come, but at peace with our decision and whatever the outcome would be.

Earlier than expected, we got word the surgery was complete and had gone very well. As we went to the seventh-floor waiting area to meet the surgeon, we actually hopped on the same elevator as Fulton heading to ICU. He was sleeping peacefully and was breathing on his own, despite still being intubated. We arrived at our floor and he continued up a few more to where we would meet him in a short bit. The surgeon soon arrived and presented us with X-rays. He pulled out the image showing Fulton's new spine.

"Look at this."

"Wow!" Tony and I gasped in unison.

"It's so straight!" I said.

"I don't think any of us thought we could get it this straight, but his bones were good and everything went really well," the surgeon replied.

We continued to gawk at the X-rays. The before image showed his spine curved and misshapen, the next showed it stick-straight and punctuated by screws and rods that would hold him in this new position until the spine finished fusing.

In the coming days, as Fulton woke up and started the difficult recovery period, I became more amazed at my son's resilience and realized that, even in tough times, God provides the strength to go on.

The recovery was extremely painful for Fulton, and I suffered watching him suffer. I grew frustrated that there was only so much I could do to help him be comfortable, and that sometimes what needed to be done to aid recovery (sit him up in his wheelchair for a couple of hours at a time) would actually cause him more pain in the first couple of weeks. When he cried and asked for pain medication, he would inevitably ask when he would feel better.

As the nurse or I quickly administered powerful pain medicine, I asked, "Fulton, do you remember how much your back hurt when you were still in the hospital?"

"Yes," he'd reply, momentarily distracted.

"I know your back hurts now, but does it hurt as bad as it did then?"

"No," he realized. "It hurts less."

"Does your back hurt as much as two days ago, when you tried going outside?"

"No, it doesn't hurt that much either," and his face softened.

"Fulton, every day it will hurt less," I said as I rubbed his legs. "It's a long recovery, but you won't be in this much pain the whole time. It will get better a little every day, and then you'll finally feel the way you did before the surgery."

• • •

I did not suffer through back surgery, but I spent many, many months in pain, believing that I would always feel that way. God was there, trying to comfort me and let me know things would get better, but for so long I refused to believe him. Now I am fully recovered. I can look back and realize, slowly but surely, that by being faithful even when it was hard, God was healing my hurt. I probably slowed down the process at times by not listening, or doing what I thought was best, but when I see Fulton now happily speeding around the yard in his power chair, tall and proud, I realize I too am walking taller with the weight of grief and despair lifted off my shoulders. I can look to the future with hope, rather than worry, and can trust that, regardless of whatever else happens, I can make it through. Proper planning, guided by prudence, and not some misguided idea that I can control everything, means my marriage is on track, my self-care is on track, and the care of my children is providing them with the room to grow, thrive, and achieve whatever God has in store for them. Fulton and Teddy may never be priests or professional football players, but God has a unique mission for both of them that I'm excited to watch unfold.

In the more than ten years since we received Fulton's diagnosis, Tony and I have experienced the highest highs and lowest lows, experience teaching us that the roller coaster ride will probably have many more rises and falls to come. Nevertheless, neither of us could deny how blessed we were. We are not saints or superheroes, but we learned to endure by enjoying each day, trusting in God and his plan, accepting help from others, being grateful, and loving each other more through each sacrifice. If people looked at us and felt pity, that was their problem. We had discovered a joy and peace that comes when you realize you're not in control, but that everything will be OK anyway. Our strength came from years of prayer, tears, heartache, and hope; and now with renewed faith, we could trust God unfailingly. Every day is joyful. Every day is a gift. Every day I can thank God from the bottom of my heart. Everything isn't perfect, but thankfully I learned it doesn't have to be.

## What You Can Do: Planning Prudently Instead of Worrying

Worrying about and planning for the future are two separate things. By prayerfully planning, you can eliminate most of the worry that comes from making big, and sometimes scary, life-changing decisions. Educate yourself as much as possible so you will know you did the best you could, and can trust God with the details. That leaves room for you to enjoy each moment rather than focus on the what-ifs. However, don't just throw your hands up and leave it all to God! That's not trust, that's avoidance. Recognize when you're avoiding important decisions out of fear. Every time you find yourself avoiding making a plan, ask yourself if you'd prefer to figure this out when your child is struggling in the emergency department. In emergencies and crisis, having plans laid out in advance will eliminate confusion and second-guessing. In some cases, having legally binding documents ready in advance will make sure your wishes, or those of your child, are followed if you are not present.

Your child's spiritual health may also require some forethought. Thankfully, there are more resources and awareness today than previously for preparing special-needs children for the sacraments. However, give your parish plenty of notice if your child requires special accommodations. Your parish may not be aware of what special programs and accommodations are available or necessary. Educate yourself so you can advocate for your child's spiritual well-being.

If you have disabled and non-disabled children, your parenting and planning will look different for each, and that's OK. Be honest with your special-needs kids, but don't worry them with grim future statistics. You don't know what new medical intervention may arise between now and then, so be realistic, but leave room for possibility. Allow them to help with planning as much as they are able to so they can grow to advocate and speak out for themselves, as well as find friends and companions who will join in supporting them as you get older.

---

## KEY TAKEAWAYS

- Avoiding tough decisions doesn't make them go away, it only increases your worry.
- Educating yourself and making time to plan for the future mean decisions aren't made in the heat of the moment.

- A well-thought-out plan means you can enjoy more time with your child and trust God with the unexpected details.
- Your child has a right to the sacraments. Make sure you understand how your child can be accommodated so you can assist your parish leaders if they are unaware of the best way to proceed.
- Strive to raise confident kids who can advocate for themselves as they get older.

## Asking for Wisdom Like King Solomon

When seeking guidance on how to plan wisely for our children's futures, we need only turn to the words of King Solomon in the Old Testament for inspiration. In a dream, when asked what gift he wanted from God, Solomon replied:

> And now, O LORD my God, you have made your servant king in place of David my father, Although, I am but a little child; I do not know how to go out or come in. And your servant is in the midst of your people whom you have chosen, a great people, that cannot be numbered of counted for multitude. Give your servant therefore an understanding mind to govern your people, that I may discern between good and evil; for who is able to govern this great people of yours? (1 Kings 3:7–9)

Just as we realize that we often feel overwhelmed in our duties, we also recognize we are here, set before this giant task, because God trusts us with it. Let us ask him for a discerning heart and the ability to distinguish between right and wrong, so that we may leave aside worry and find peace in our vocation.

# Conclusion

Tony and I drove down a narrow small-town street that ended at a yard beside a cute brick ranch house. We parked across the street from the house with a For Sale By Owner sign in the yard and walked up the driveway to meet the seller for a tour. We exchanged pleasantries and the man, who was the son-in-law of the deceased owners, pushed a button on a remote and the garage door opened.

"Now that ramp would be easy to remove," he quickly said. "It's only attached at a couple spots around the door frame."

Tony and I were flabbergasted, and both quickly started talking over top of one another. "No, that's fine." "That ramp is great!" "We need a ramp anyway!" And we quickly explained our unique family needs. We eagerly toured the house. Despite being completed in 1962 (by the deceased owner himself, who was a brick mason), the doorways were wide, as was the hallway to the bedrooms. The master bathroom would require minimal renovations to work with the boys' bath chair. If the boys needed anything in the middle of the night, we would only need to walk across a hall, rather than down the steps and to the other side of the house. Plus, there was space for a library schoolroom, and Tony could have an office in the basement. The driveway was paved! Only a short walk from the front door was a small town with a cute main street. We could walk to a Catholic church with an adoration chapel, an Italian grocery store, and a train station that could take Tony into Philadelphia for work. It seemed almost too good to be true. Could this house really be the answer to our prayers?

Weeks after Fulton's surgery, Teddy still needed to sleep in the living room, and it was looking more and more unlikely that we'd be able to move his bed back into the bedroom he had shared with Fulton. Transferring Fulton from his wheelchair to his bed and back again required at least two people and plenty of space, something that room did not have with two hospital beds in it. Despite being able to make do for ten years in our house, we'd reached a point where it was either construct a huge addition or move. Ideally we wanted to move to a one-level house, and now that Tony had a new job, it was a possibility, but we still had a very strict budget and a long list of needs. It seemed unlikely we'd find anything that suited our needs and was in our price range. And then I saw the listing for the brick ranch.

We settled on an absolute offer we couldn't go over. We presented the offer, but asked that we be allowed to come through again with our sons so we could see how they navigated the house. The sellers agreed to let our family come through, and together the two daughters of the previous owners agreed to sell us their parents' home. It has suited us perfectly ever since our move in January 2019.

When we had purchased our previous home the year Fulton

was born, it was supposed to be our forever home. But that 1920s bungalow with a long gravel driveway was not what ultimately worked for our family. We made it work for a long time, made many wonderful memories there, but we couldn't stay in that house. A brick ranch house in a small town was something completely different, but it's perfect for our family. I often wonder, if we didn't have two sons with SMA, how would our life look? Would we still live in our old house? What decisions would we have made differently throughout the years? I'm sure our life would have been filled with challenges, just different challenges. But of course, my life is the one I just wrote about in this book. Although I'm in a different place mentally, spiritually, and even geographically than I was before we started down this journey, my life is filled with joy, even though it looks nothing like I thought it would as I carried baby Fulton into his new house in the summer of 2008.

We simply can't imagine all the ways our family can be happy, and so often our view of a joyful life is limited by our own experiences. When we are blessed with a special-needs child, God is not trying to ruin our plans. He is trying to broaden our horizons. He is asking you to leave behind your preconceived notions and trust that, with this child in your life, you will not only be OK, you will be better than OK, and your days will be as joyful as they were before, even if things look completely different. I wake up every day and thank God for a life I didn't even know could exist, for a life I didn't think I wanted. Now I don't doubt his plan, and I'm hopeful for the future, whatever it looks like. I know the same can be true for you too.

# Acknowledgments

This book was created for all the Catholic special-needs parents out there who trusted me enough to reach out and ask questions. Without their correspondence, I never would have known this book needed to be written. Thank you for sharing your stories with me and encouraging me to share more of my own.

For more than nine years, people from all over the world have visited my website time and time again to read my blog posts, be they funny, serious, or downright ridiculous. The support of my dedicated readers helped me find my voice and write my way through my own healing process. When I'm tired, uninspired, and unwilling to sit down at my computer, my readers always step up with words of support and encouragement, and have motivated me to keep writing (whether they knew it or not). I never would have considered writing a book if I didn't have so many wonderful people cheering me on from behind their screens.

To all the special-needs moms who supported me through the years, even when I was resistant to embracing my vocation, and who continue to inspire me with their words and actions, especially Shelby Myers, Mary Lenaburg, Traci High, and Rebecca Frech. I am blessed by your friendships.

While drinking gin and tonics for my birthday, Jennifer Fulwiler told me I had a story to tell and I needed to make sure I told it before I possibly went down in a fiery plane crash. Thank you for being a great inspiration and lighting a fire under me to get this book written.

Heidi Hess Saxton saw the potential in my idea and helped it become an even better book than I imagined. With help from Our Sunday Visitor editors Rebecca Martin and Mary Beth Giltner, this idea was brought to fruition, and we created a book better than anything I could have imagined. Thank you, ladies, for using your talents to improve my own.

In 2013 several Catholic bloggers came together to create a private Facebook group. We didn't even know what a mastermind group was, but born from our desire to be better bloggers came real friendship and valuable advice not limited to blogging or books. Haley, Christy, Kendra, Bonnie, Abbey, Sarah, Mandi, and Molly: Thank you for your ongoing friendship, support, and honesty.

To my Mater and CHAPLET families, you supported us spiritually and physically through the toughest of days. I don't know how we would have made it through without our faith community pulling for us. And to Theresa and Kori, thank you especially for always understanding my sense of humor, even in the darkest of times.

To my in-laws, Domenic and Cheryl, you always stepped up and stepped in when we needed help. Thank you for always welcoming every new blessing with unconditional love.

To my parents, Roger and Patti, thank you for loving me no matter what, encouraging me to always follow my dreams, and being my original cheerleaders.

Adeline, Byron, Edith, Fulton, and Theodore: I am the woman I am today because of you all. You make me want to be a better person every day, and continually amaze me by being the greatest kids a mother could ever want, despite all my parenting flaws. Although I have been your teacher for many years, each of you teaches me, and stretches me to grow, in ways I never could have imagined. I hope I make you as proud of me as I am of each of you.

Tony, you have been the steadfast rock of our family through everything, and without you I'd be lost. Thank you for always supporting and encouraging my writing, and making sacrifices when necessary so I could write this book. Thank you for allowing me to share our story. I pray we have many more years, and many more stories to share.

# Appendix 1
# How to Help the Special-Needs Families in Your Life

For those reading this book who do not have a special-needs child, you may be wondering how you can help those families in your parish or community who do. Whether you know the family personally or only casually, there are lots of ways you can help without being pushy.

**Prayer**
I know you want to do more. Sometimes prayer often doesn't seem like enough in light of what your friend or loved one is facing, but prayer is the most important thing you can offer. When I was too angry to pray, it was the prayers of others that filled the gaps. When I was too scared to say more than a Hail Mary, the prayers of others told God of my sorrows and hopes. In the

toughest times, when God was certainly giving me more than I could handle on my own, I felt the prayers of my community strengthening and supporting me to keep going.

Ask for specific prayer requests, and follow up on them. Even when things may seem to be going well, ask if there is something you should be praying for. Special-needs parents learn to hide their daily challenges; you might be surprised to learn how hard things have been, when on the outside everything looks fine.

### Lend a Listening Ear

Learn to simply listen without saying anything. You don't need to offer advice, and a phrase you think may be uplifting could actually send the opposite message. You don't need to try to relate to what they're going through. In fact, they will probably prefer that you admit you have no idea what it must be like for them. Just let the parent talk and vent to you without judgment, and if possible, be strong for them. Don't break down uncontrollably, no matter how hard the news is to hear. Hold them while they cry. Don't create a situation in which they need to turn from their own worry and grief to support you. If you can provide a strong shoulder, you will be a valuable asset to any special-needs parent.

### Offer Aid for Specific Needs

As you pray and listen, you will learn of specific needs that a family is facing.

Consider offering aid, either financial or in other tangible ways, such as providing meals or child care during a hospitalization. You could offer to set up an Amazon Wishlist of items that people can purchase for the family, or organize a fundraiser to offset a medical expense. However, don't offer to run a spaghetti dinner if you have no idea how to go about doing so and aren't sure you have the time to find out. You don't have to plan big events and raise tons of money to make a difference in the lives of a special-needs family. Often there are many small needs a family wouldn't necessarily think to ask for (help with housekeeping, running errands, child care, school drop-offs and pick-ups, grocery shopping, etc.). If the family does need a large amount of money raised, help them find someone who does have experience organizing crowdfunding pages and fundraising events. Also consider just asking people to donate money rather than setting up a restaurant fundraiser (in which the restaurant will take a cut) or selling something that people may not want. Give people an option to just donate money rather than spend it on items. Many charity T-shirts line the racks of Goodwill!

Don't assume you know what a family needs. I've had very well-meaning people offer to give us money when there was no need, or wrote letters on our behalf to ask for equipment we couldn't use. Please, always check with a family, no matter how good you feel your intentions are.

Accepting help from others requires humility, and it can be hard for families who have never needed help to suddenly find themselves unable to provide for their child. Don't get angry if a family refuses your help. Keep offering specific aid and eventually your help will be accepted.

## Teach Acceptance

Most parents fear their children will stare or say something rude when meeting a disabled person for the first time. If you want your child to accept special-needs individuals, start exposing them to people with different abilities from a young age. There are many books and shows that now include disabled children and adult characters.

If your child sees someone in public using a wheelchair or guide dog, or with some other noticeable impairment, don't shush them and pull them away. Simply treat the person as you would anyone else; smile and say hello if you normally would, and encourage your child to do the same.

Understand that not every public encounter is a teachable moment; the disabled person does not need to answer questions, and you don't need to go out of your way to point out disabled people to your child. If your child has a question, answer it if you're able, ask the person if they're willing, or look it up later online.

Avoid saying things like "something is wrong" or "that person is sick." A disabled person is living a normal life, even if it doesn't seem normal to you or your child. You can tell your child, "That man/woman/child is disabled and uses a wheelchair/cane/walker/guide dog to help him/her self." If your child associates using a specialized device as something negative, you can stress that the device is actually a good thing because it gives the person more freedom to get around on their own.

Don't patronize or assume someone is intellectually delayed.

Make sure your child knows to never touch someone's medical equipment, not even a guide dog. Explain that these things are an extension of the person, and touching their wheelchair, dog, crutches, etc. is an invasion of that person's personal space.

Well-meaning Catholics need to understand that many disabled adults do not want strangers randomly coming up to them and offering prayers for a cure. The fact that someone is disabled is not a sign that they, or their parents, or someone else did something wrong, or that God has chosen to ignore their prayers. Just because you can't imagine spending life in a wheelchair doesn't mean the disabled person is unhappy. A cure or miracle is often a welcome blessing, but it does not mean someone is spiritually better than someone else. Not getting a cure doesn't mean someone's a bigger sinner than anyone else. We're all still sinners!

## If You Are in Ministry

If you are a priest, director of religious education, youth ministry leader, or someone in a position of leadership at your parish, there are a few extra things you can do. The United States Conference of Catholic Bishops states the following:

> It is essential that all forms of the liturgy be completely accessible to persons with disabilities, since these forms are the essence of the spiritual tie that binds the Christian community together. To exclude members of the parish from these celebrations of the life of the Church, even by passive omission, is to deny the reality of that community. Accessibility involves far more than physical alterations to parish buildings. Realistic provision must be made for Catholics with disabilities to participate fully in the Eucharist and other liturgical celebrations. (*Guidelines for the Celebration of the Sacraments with Persons with Disabilities (Revised Edition)*)

***Consider how you can make church buildings more accessible so that Mass and other liturgical observances (Stations of the Cross, adoration, etc.) can be attended by all.***

- Where can people in wheelchairs sit during a service?
- How easy is it for them to receive Communion or view a baptism?
- Do you have blind or hard-of-hearing parishioners? Are they able to understand the Mass?
- How could you accommodate children and adults who may have vocal outbursts during Mass, or who are unable to sit still?

In this day and age, people shouldn't need to cut a hole in the ceiling and lower someone down to get close to Our Lord.

***Make parish events (fish fry, pancake breakfasts, picnics, etc.) accessible.***

If the church hall is in the basement without an elevator, you're excluding anyone with a mobility challenge from attending functions held there. You can't say everyone is invited to participate in parish life and ministries if a large chunk of the building is off limits. Consider finding a new location for events.

*Make the sacraments accessible.*
Every church member should be considered when determining where and when sacraments are offered, as well as the sacramental preparations:

> Pastors are responsible to provide evangelization, catechetical formation, and sacramental preparation for parishioners with disabilities, and dioceses are encouraged to establish appropriate support services to assist pastors in this duty. Persons with disabilities, their advocates and their families, as well as those knowledgeable in serving those with disabilities, can make a most valuable contribution to these efforts. Parish catechetical and sacramental preparation programs may need to be adapted for some parishioners with disabilities, though, as much as possible, persons with disabilities should be integrated into the ordinary programs. They should not be segregated for specialized catechesis unless their disabilities make it impossible for them to participate in the basic catechetical program. Even in those cases, participation in parish life is encouraged in all ways possible. (*Guidelines for the Celebration of the Sacraments with Persons with Disabilities (Revised Edition)*)

*Consider the health and needs of individual parish members, rather than simply parish policy, when determining how and when to administer the sacraments.*

- If there is a risk of a child dying prematurely, offer the sacraments sooner.
- If the child cannot attend the standard sacramental prep classes, help guide the family with home instruction, or see if the diocese offers assistance.
- Talk to parents or find diocesan supports to learn the best ways to modify or change your parish's CCD programs to meet the needs of your disabled parishioners, and seek out catechetical supplies that are designed for children with special needs.
- Make religious education classrooms accessible or move classes to a different location in your building. If the child needs a bathroom break, is there a suitable bathroom near the classrooms?

### The welcome wagon

To get a sense of how accessible and welcoming your parish is to a person with a disability, do a walk-through with the disabled members of your parish and listen to their concerns. Chances are you are not even aware of the problems they face in attending Mass, CCD, or parish events. Even if your parish meets the minimum for Americans with Disabilities Act compliance, chances are there are parts of the building that are inaccessible. Ramps, automatic doors, larger bathroom stalls — make your church more accessible for everyone, not just the disabled.

In addition to accessibility issues, disabled Catholics and their families face many hurdles in attending Mass. Almost one-third of parents surveyed in a 2013 study of 400 special-needs families said they had left at least one church because their child was not included or welcomed.[*] A 2014 study found that people with disabilities are less likely to attend worship services and

---

[*]https://meridian.allenpress.com/idd/article-abstract/51/1/48/6263/Congregational-Participa-tion-and-Supports-for?

other church activities than non-disabled people.[*] A 2013 study found that more than half of the surveyed special-needs parents reported that their child with a disability had been excluded at church.[†]

Creating an accessible parish doesn't end with a new ramp or elevator. To truly serve disabled Catholics and their families, Catholic parishes need to become educated as to the best ways to welcome and include those who are autistic, blind, intellectually delayed, hard-of-hearing, physically disabled, and those whose condition defies diagnosis yet offers its own struggles. View some of the resources in Appendix 2 for help.

[*]Eleanor X. Liu, Erik W. Carter, L. Thomas, Naomi H. Annandale, Courtney E. Taylor, "In Their Own Words: The Place of Faith in the Lives of Young People With Autism and Intellectual Disability," Intellectual and Developmental Disabilities 52, no. 5 (October 2014): 388-404.

[†]Elizabeth O'Hanlon, "Religion and Disability: The Experiences of Families of Children with Special Needs," Journal of Religion, Disability & Health 17, no. 1 (2013).

# Appendix 2
# Resources

**Blogs**

www.thisaintthelyceum.org

    The inspiration and precursor to this book, I write about all the joy (and chaos) life with five kids — including two with special needs — creates on a regular basis.

www.emilymdeardo.com

    Author Emily DeArdo is a double-lung transplant survivor who lives with cystic fibrosis. She writes about books, faith, and living *memento mori*.

www.faithfulnotsuccessful.com

    Christy Wilkens is a homeschooling mother of six who writes about Catholic family life and being a special-needs mom to her youngest son, Oscar.

https://mustardseedsandwildflowers.wordpress.com
Mandy Mazzawi is a mother of three who writes about Catholic family life, including special-needs parenting.

www.notsoformulaic.com
Ginny Kochis is a mom who seeks to help other moms of twice-exceptional or differently wired kids. She offers creative advice and activities to aid learning.

www.patheos.com/blogs/throughcatholiclenses
Fr. Matthew P. Schneider, LC, is a priest with the Legionaries of Christ and Regnum Christi. He is autistic and writes about the Catholic Faith and disability.

www.sweepingupjoy.com
Alicia Schonhardt writes about homeschooling, family life, and how to tackle the hard times around her daughter's diagnosis of systemic-onset juvenile idiopathic arthritis.

www.sylcell.com
Sylvia Bass is a mom to six, including a daughter with Down syndrome. She writes about Catholic family life and the lessons she has learned as a special-needs mom.

www.thisspecialjourney.com
On her blog, Kate Anderson shares an honest look at life with three special-needs children.

www.workandplaydaybyday.com
Heidi Indahl is a homeschooler who shares advice on home education for special-needs children, as well as resources for poor prenatal diagnosis and pregnancy/infant loss.

## Books

Kathryn Anne Casey, *Journey in Love: A Catholic Mother's Prayers after Prenatal Diagnosis* (Our Sunday Visitor, 2019).

Christina Chase, *It Is Good To Be Here: A Disabled Woman's Reflections on God in the Flesh and the Sacred Wonder of Being Human* (Sophia Institute Press, 2019).

Michele E. Chronister, *Handbook for Adaptive Catechesis: Serving Those with Special Needs* (Liguori Publications, 2012).

Michele E. Chronister, *Taking the Lift to Heaven: The Pocket Guide to Adaptive Ministry in Your Catholic Parish* (CreateSpace, 2016).

Emily M. DeArdo, *Living Memento Mori: My Journey through the Stations of the Cross* (Ave Maria Press, 2020).

Randy Hain, *Special Children, Blessed Fathers: Encouragement for Fathers of Children with Special Needs* (Emmaus Road Publishing, 2015).

Charleen Katra, *The Adaptive Teacher: Faith-Based Strategies to Reach and Teach Learners with Disabilities* (Loyola Press, 2019).

Debra Kelsey-Davis and Kelly Johnson, *The Caregiver's Companion: A Christ-Centered Journal to Nourish Your Soul* (Ave Maria Press, 2020).

Mary E. Lenaburg, *Be Brave in the Scared: How I Learned to Trust God during the Most Difficult Days of My Life* (Ave Maria Press, 2019).

Maureen Pratt, *Salt and Light: Church, Disability, and the Blessing of Welcome for All* (Twenty-Third Publications, 2018).

David Rizzo, *Faith, Family, and Children with Special Needs: How Catholic Parents and Their Kids with Special Needs Can Develop a Richer Spiritual Life* (Loyola Press, 2012).

David Rizzo and Mercedes McBride Rizzo, *Spiritually Able: A Parent's Guide to Teaching the Faith to Children with Special Needs* (Loyola Press, 2015).

David and Mercedes Rizzo, *Praying for Your Special Needs Child* (Word Among Us Press, 2018).

Nancy Huber-Anthony Schuerger, *A Catechist's Handbook for Children Who Are Deaf or Hard of Hearing* (Catholic Office Of the

Deaf, 1999).

Lawrence R. Sutton, Ph.D., *How to Welcome, Include, and Catechize Children with Autism and Other Special Needs: A Parish-Based Approach* (Loyola Press, 2013).

Joseph D. White, Ph.D., and Ana Arista White, *Catechists for All Children* (Our Sunday Visitor, 2002).

## Other Religious Education Materials

Charleen Katra, *How to Talk to Children About People with Disabilities*, pamphlet (Twenty-Third Publications, 2019).

David and Mercedes Rizzo, *The Adaptive First Eucharist Preparation Kit* (Loyola Press, 2011).

Joseph D. White, Ph.D., *The Way God Teaches: Special Needs*, pamphlet (Our Sunday Visitor, 2015).

Joseph D. White, Ph.D., *Catechist's Companion: Multisensory Methods in Catechesis*, pamphlet (Our Sunday Visitor, 2007).

## Organizations

National Catholic Bioethics Center: www.ncbcenter.org

National Catholic Board on Full Inclusion:
   https://fullinclusionforcatholicschools.org/

National Catholic Partnership on Disability: www.ncpd.org

National Catholic Office for the Deaf: http://ncod.org/

## Websites, Etc.

Accepting the Gift, Online Apostolate for Catholic Special Needs Parents: acceptingthegift.org

Accepting the Gift Facebook Group: www.facebook.com /groups/404206513568962/

Autism Consecrated: https://autismconsecrated.com/

Autism With the Rizzos: www.davidandmercedesrizzo.com/

Autistic Priest Youtube Channel: www.youtube.com/channel/ UCaA9aN7_YQMAnk9secXwZmw

Catholic Parents Raising Special Needs Kids Facebook Group: www.facebook.com/groups/312170262240382/

Nourish for Caregivers, A support group for caregivers.: https://nourishforcaregivers.com/

# About the Author

Kelly Mantoan is a Catholic convert, wife, mother to five, home-schooler, and special-needs parent. She writes about her faith, family, homeschooling, and special-needs parenting at her popular blog *This Ain't the Lyceum*. In 2019 Kelly started a conference and online apostolate for Catholic special-needs parents. Accepting the Gift provides support and resources that can help Catholic special-needs parents thrive in their unique vocation.

# Parenting Your Kids with Grace
(Birth to Age 10)

*Dr. Greg and Lisa Popcak*
T2363 | 978-1-68192-481-6

Believe it or not, the Catholic family isn't primarily a human institu-
tion. It's a divine one. By uniting
with the sacramental life of the
Church, your common, ordinary,
crazy family becomes something
sacred, a "domestic church."

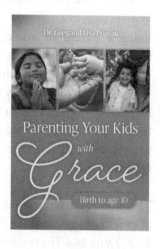

Family therapist and parent Greg-
ory Popcak and his wife, Lisa, are
back with *Parenting Your Kids with
Grace*. Building on their best-selling book *Parenting with Grace*, first
published twenty years ago, this new volume draws on the same
parenting principles and provides up-to-date research to guide
parents through each stage of child development from birth to
age ten.

# Parenting Your Teens and Tweens with Grace
(Ages 11 to 18)

*Dr. Greg and Lisa Popcak*
T2376 | 978-1-68192-485-4

Being a parent of adolescents is tough work. Trying to raise faithful teens and tweens can seem like an impossible mission. Today's Catholic parents need access to the best tools and most up-to-date research to help them fully cooperate with God's grace.

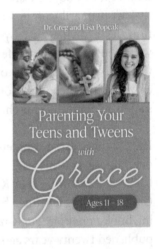

That's what Dr. Greg and Lisa Popcak seek to help you do in *Parenting Your Teens and Tweens with Grace*. Building on their best-selling book *Parenting with Grace*, this new volume guides parents on how to raise preteens and teenagers with grace and joy.